Cougar Dating

How To Land The Perfect Cougar.

Tips and Tricks For Younger Men Looking For Older Women.

by
Lucy Lumbarton

I0150032

Contents

Introduction

'He said he thought I was about twenty; which is still too young, but not running-from-the-law young.' – Kirsten Reed

Over time, dating norms have changed. What was considered taboo a few decades ago may now be the "in" thing. Society has certainly progressed in more than one way, and one aspect that most men are ecstatic about is the ability to date older women without being frowned upon!

It's a freeing notion for both men and women alike and allows both sexes to be free to mix and mingle as they please. After all, who wouldn't want a beauty like Demi Moore by their side to flaunt to their friends?

While it may initially seem daunting, finding and keeping an older woman is not as difficult as it is cracked up to be. In this guide, we're going to walk you through each process of how to win over such a woman, take you step by step and show you, so that you can be on your way to dating that older woman of your dreams in no time!

What you'll need is confidence, dating knowledge, tips and tricks that work in your favour, and the ability to understand a cougar's psyche.

Let's face it guys, while you may have your chiselled body, good looks, and young age on your side, an older woman is more experienced and needs to be wowed beyond what a younger female is likely to fall for – she needs you to challenge her and show her the man that you really are. That is after all what she is looking for, a strong male and not a wimpy boy toy lover.

This dating guide articulates in a crystal clear fashion what older women are looking for in their younger beau. If this is your first time and you find yourself really falling for an older woman don't be intimidated by the prospect of going up to her and asking her out for a date.

Yes, while the delightful Mrs Robinson can at first play hard to get, a little patience and a little understanding on your part of just what she *needs* will definitely have her swooning at your feet.

So the games you play with girls your age will not necessarily work on older women. That's why we have written this book; to spell out the right moves to make and the right things to say to an older woman, all to win her heart over and make her yours. So if you're looking to spice things up in your life and find an older woman to be with, you've come to the right place!

Dating an older woman has never been this easy because we have put forth all the details you need to bag that cougar everyone else has been eyeing. Just make sure you read this book carefully from beginning to end, you won't regret it when you've got her by your side.

Chapter Walk Through

The term 'cougar' has been misunderstood since the day it was first coined and it has been used with a negative connotation. As Cougar Life founder Claudia Opdenkelder emphasised, when it comes to the term, people have to embrace it and take the term and make it their own. This is how the negative association of the term can be taken and made to mean a whole new thing. In chapter one of this book we look at these common misconceptions and how to break them.

Chapter One also takes a look at the popular cougars in recent culture and gives a brief history and background of how cultural stereotypes are changing. If you want to be surprised by how much the world's ideas have changed and are changing, then keep reading.

Chapter Two looks at the advantages that cougars can expect when they date younger men. It gives cubs the opportunity to see life from a cougar's point of view and what they bring to the table when they enter the relationship.

Chapter Three focuses on the disadvantages that cougars face which accompanies being associated with younger men. Choosing the cougar lifestyle isn't going to be a walk in the park and in this chapter, we attempt to break down what a lot of older women face when they enter these relationships and how it is likely to affect you.

Chapter Four takes a look at the advantages that younger men can expect to enjoy when they go out with older women and the numerous benefits that are part and parcel of such a coupling. Cubs, it is a good idea to know just what to anticipate from such a relationship and how to choose the best cougar for you.

Chapter Five delves into the downside of cougar/cub couplings and opens your eyes to the reality of the situation, the ups and downs that will be the result of your relationship and how you can best overcome all the negative things you may encounter.

In Chapter Six we bring you all the wonderful websites where you can find cougars waiting to be romanced. We will also discuss other places where you can meet and find cougars.

Chapter Seven takes you by the hand and literally walks you step by step through the process of finding a cougar. How do you capture the attention of a woman who knows what she wants? How do you make her say yes to your demands? How do your tame this cougar? Chapter Seven holds the secrets to this.

Chapter Eight congratulates you on successfully capturing a cougar, so now that she has accepted your advances and is now yours, how do you get her to stay? Read on to find out more.

Chapter Nine takes cougar/cub couples to a whole new level as it discusses the potential clash in lifestyle issues and how to address them. If you want your relationship to last with her, then you definitely don't want to skip this chapter.

Chapter 1) The Cougar Defined

Of course, we all initially thought of the animal when we first heard the term cougar, but in today's day and age, a woman described as a "cougar" is someone who seeks sexual relations with considerably younger men. While sex may not be the first thing on her mind, it's definitely not the last. A cougar is on the PROWL for younger men, younger men such as you who are up for the challenge.
****

The term cougar was initially used to describe an older and more experienced woman who enjoys having sexual relations with a man considerably younger than herself. This doesn't mean that she is a slut; neither does it mean she is desperate. It simply shows that she enjoys offering sexual expertise and is open to new ideas and experiences.
****

You just have to make sure that you're prepared when the opportunity knocks on your door because even the slightest hesitation or a wrong move can send a cougar away.

The word cougar began being used as slang in Western Canada and was first seen on a Canadian dating website known as Cougardate.com.

While there is no hard and fast rule as to how young of a male cougars are looking for, we've seen men as young as 20 years less than a woman's age get picked up. We've also seen that women, who are over the age of 40, aggressively desire and pursue sexual relations with men in their 20s or 30s. A cougar is looking for you. You just have to be visible to her in public and be ready to sweep her off her feet when she comes your way.

Breaking Cougar Stereotypes – Two Kinds of Women
****

The description of a cougar is a woman who is extremely self-confident and self-assured who knows exactly what it is that she wants.

'If as a woman you find yourself on the fence about this, then perfhaps you aren't the kind of person who should be looking into developing this kind of lifestyle, because being a cougar isn't about following a trend, it's a lifestyle.' – Claudia Opdenkelder, founder of Cougar Life Dating Service
****

The most common stereotype that comes across when people hear the word 'cougar' is that of a power hungry, sex deprived woman in her 40s. The truth is that the majority of women who find themselves in these relationships never deliberately went out looking for these men. It was rather the men who approached them and pursued them.

This is because women in general, just as society in general are still stuck with the mindset that makes them feel like they are committing a sin and engaging in something that is taboo when they find themselves in such relationships. Oftentimes the women who are not comfortable about going out with younger men need more than a one-time proposal to convince them to go out with them.

A classic example is Pauletta Pearson, Denzel Washington's wife. She is four years his senior and needed to be asked three times before she agreed to marry him. They have been happily married for more than 30 years now.

If you do meet with such a woman, know that she may genuinely like you for who you are, but is fighting the right and wrong battle in her own mind. Give her time and space to make up her own mind.

Then on the other spectrum of the cougar scale you have women who are raring to go. Cougars that are in the dating game 100% and don't give a hoot about society norms and customs. These women are great fun because they like living life to the fullest and will live and let live.

How Should You Approach Each Type?

Essentially at the heart of every woman is the desire to be loved and cherished. How you do this is up to you but know that in as much as a man desires to be affirmed and respected, the same is true for women across every race, creed and culture. All women want to be loved and cherished, yes cougars too.

Whether the woman is a passive cougar or an aggressive cougar, this is the underlying thread that you need to keep in mind when you begin pursuing her.

- **The passive cougar**

The passive cougar may not be deliberately throwing herself out onto the dating scene, perhaps she is the single mum next door, or your lovely co-worker who just happens to be the hottest boss lady you have ever met, regardless of where you meet her, if she is not putting herself onto the market you need to be careful how you approach and start the conversations.

Build a friendship first before you ask her out otherwise you risk getting stuck in a highly awkward situation. Get to know her more and what she likes. And slowly with time you can make your intentions known to her.

She may reject you the first time, but don't lose hope remember she is fighting her thoughts and what she thinks society at large will think of her.

- **The aggressive cougar**

The aggressive cougar is nothing short of a flirt and delights in watching you squirm as you try to win her heart. She will play with your heart and toy with it before saying yes. She knows she can have any suitor she wants and so she enjoys playing games before she allows herself to be caught. She embodies the sentiment of playing hard to get and enjoys teasing you.

She is a master at seducing men and she doesn't care what people say really. She knows what she wants and she isn't intimidated by society's double standards. 'What is good for the gander is certainly good for the goose as well' is her motto.

You will find her trawling all the cougar dating websites flaunting her best assets which she is fully aware you cannot resist. Her charm and beauty is unrivalled and she knows she looks younger that she really is. And more often than not, she *always* gets what she wants.

Cougar Dating Statistics
****

A 2013 US Population Survey showing the age difference in heterosexual married couples demonstrated that of the entire population of married people living in the US at the time of the survey, 6.5% of couples the wife was 2-3 years older than the husband compared to 20.4% of husbands who were 2-3 years older than their wives.

Where the wife was 4-5 years older than the husband this affected only 3.3% of the entire married population.

0.3% is the percentage of entire marriages where the wife was 20+ years older than the husband.
****

Since time memorial the socially accepted norm and custom when it comes to dating and marriage was that the man must be older than the woman. It didn't really matter if the man was a day older or ten years older, just so long as he was older it was considered fine. This age old custom had been so ingrained in people's minds that a formula had even been invented to determine a suitable age for a bride to get married. The rule stated that a man was free to wed a girl so long as her age equaled or was greater than his age plus seven.

Thankfully this is no longer the case and men are free to engage with adult women of their liking irrespective of their age. After all, what is age but just a number right?

It's refreshing to see how these ancient outdated norms are being challenged with people exercising their freedom to follow their heart instead of letting themselves be held back by societal norms.

This trend of women opting to pursue relations with younger men, and younger men proceeding to not only date but marry these women has increased greatly over the years.

Studies conducted in the United Kingdom in 2003 showed that between 1963 and 1998 there was an 11% rise in the number of women who chose to get married to men significantly younger than themselves.

That's not all, in the same year, an AARP study also showed that 34% of women over the age of 39 years were engaged in relations with younger men.
This is good news boys!

Not only are women breaking forth from the chains that have held them back and societies' repressive thinking which has told them to keep their feelings for younger men hidden, but they are getting out there with a vengeance! There are even several reality TV series that have been filmed that aim to show people just how cougar/cub relationships are like any other relationships.

These shows are designed to challenge the thinking that has long been regarded as taboo and show people that if men have been allowed to do it why shouldn't women also have the liberty to enjoy their new found freedom and love who they want, instead of being confined to men within their 'socially accepted ' age range. After all what is good for the gander should be good for the goose as well right?

Cougars in Popular Culture
The celebrity poster couple for the almost perfect cougar/cub couple definitely goes to former husband and wife Ashton Kutcher and Demi Moore. The two were together for a total of seven years, five of which they were married - 2005 to 2013.

Ashton was a young man in his twenties at the time he met 41 year old Demi Moore, 16 years his senior. It was love at well...first bite; they were having dinner with friends when they met each other. Demi gushes that they literally hit it off and talked well into the night. It was the stuff that fairy-tale romances are made of. Everything was bliss in their union, well that was until Ashton cheated, sigh.

Moving on, this doesn't overshadow other celebrity older woman/younger man couplings that are still going strong to this day.

Leading the pack we have Australian born, American based actor and actress Hugh Jackman and Deborra Lee Furness. The amazing couple have a 13 year age difference, but have successfully managed to balance out their careers and start a family together.

The couple has two children. They met on the set of a TV drama and the love struck Jackman admits he was instantly taken by her and proposed 3 ½ months later! They wed in 1996 and welcomed baby Oscar in 2000 and daughter Ava in 2006.

Another couple that have weathered the test of time and critics is Denzel Washington and his beautiful wife Pauletta Pearson. Did you know that it took Denzel three tries until Pauletta, who is four years his senior finally said yes to his proposals? Thirty-one years later with four kids this amazing couple is still going strong. This loving couple have shown that age is really nothing but a number.

Before rounding off, who can forget the delightful Julianne Moore and Bart Freundlich? With a nine year gap between them, these two decided to do things differently and took another route before finally tying the knot in 2003.

Admittedly Julianne was having cold feet and even confessed that at first one asks if this relationship even has a future. They had two children Caleb and Liv before they finally tied the knot for good. Julianne had just come out of a divorce when they first met in 1995 and says she wasn't looking for another long term commitment, but Cupid's arrow hit stuck and well, it has been a loving journey so far and looks to continue so for many years to come.

Our celebrity cougar roundup cannot possibly end without an

honourable mention of singer Cher. Come on, the lady is one hot mama and has had the boys running to her over the years. She must be doing something right. You don't believe us? Just take a look at this impressive repertoire of suitors who have passed through her hands.

Tom Cruise who is 16 years her junior, Val Kilmer 14 years younger than her and even Bon Jovi and famed guitarist Richie Sambora who is 13 years her junior. Well in total she has had over eleven younger suitors and her most recent beau is Tim Medvetz who is a proud twenty-four years younger than her. Well, that goes to show you boys, there must be something about being with an older woman that even the Hollywood legends cannot resist.

Chapter 2) Dating Advantages for The Cougar

Society has for many years dictated the norms and so called 'proper' behaviours that people are allowed to follow. Many cultures worldwide frown upon the relationships where the woman is older and the man younger. However with their new found freedom in the 21st century, cougars are on the prowl to enjoy the liberty that they have been denied for so long.

For those lucky enough to find a younger partner, here are just some of the exciting benefits that await them.

Bringing Back That Youthful Spark
You can be the missing key that will bring back that youthful spark in a woman that often gets lost over the years. Sometimes life wears a woman out and they forget how beautiful they used to be. Getting advances from a younger man can be the much needed boost a lot of women need to get them back onto the train of life and back to doing things they haven't done in a while.

You as a younger man can also be a welcome challenge, an enigma. Having perhaps been with several men who know what they want, being with you the young stallion raring to go can be a very attractive turn on for a woman in her older years. Knowing that you could have anyone you want but desire her, is beyond sexy, it's downright hot for her.

Ego Booster
Subconsciously, dating a younger man can make an older woman feel more attractive as she asks herself, why given the younger women around would you go for her. Admittedly older women who are attached to younger men are generally smoking hot! They are in better shape than most single younger women on the dating market. Nothing compares to the rush that older women get when they are with younger men, because all eyes will be on them she makes a greater effort to look good and presentable as well.

Sexual Stamina
Sex, just like a fine wine really does get better with age, and what

better way to fully enjoy love making than with an experienced pro from whom you can learn new tricks? Go in with an open mind, and let her take charge, you will be amazed by how much you didn't know.

Proceed with a keen and willing attitude, don't be afraid to experiment with these new found moves. Let your youthful zeal burst and find an outlet in the bedroom. Awaken in her the desire she has been yearning to release. Sex can be a fantastic way for the two of you to enjoy one another and discover new things together. Be prepared for some hot, fun, steamy lovemaking!

Lack of Baggage

Most men who meet an older woman and pursue a relationship with her have generally never been married before. This can mean that the man has no previous children from prior marriages or partners to speak of which can be a welcome advantage for an older woman. Cases where children are involved can in all honesty become rather complicated and so a younger man entering such a relationship without baby mamma drama is a welcome relief.

Physical Attraction

Have you ever wondered why you are particularly attracted to certain people and not by some? We meet people on a daily basis but there are some people who are very special with whom we feel a certain connection.

For us as men, attraction to a woman starts on the physical level. We like what we see and before we can even stop our minds, we have already imagined what it would be like to be in bed with such a woman. What drives us crazy as men is the thought of what she as a cougar could do to us in the bedroom. That alone sends shivers done our spine.

The advantages for a cougar are numerous. Young men want to spoil her and love her. Young men desire to learn much from her. Love, honour and respect are what await a woman willing to let a younger man woo her and sweep her off her feet.

Chapter 3) Dating Disadvantages For The Cougar

No matter how charming a young man is and how romantic he may be, and dashing, there are still a few differences that will ultimately tell us whether a relationship is meant to be or is just a fling that will be enjoyed while it lasts.

At the end of the day when all is said and done no one can tell whether a relationship will last or not, but there are some definite deal breakers that can be easily observed before the relationship even goes to the next level.

Lifestyle Differences
****

Fun for her might be a day off away from the kids, if she has kids, in order to pamper herself and feel refreshed. Or it might be a day to spring clean the house. While for you, because of your youthful energy, fun for you might consist of loud music and high intensity sports. It is good to have things that both parties can do apart from each other and together. Create that time in your schedule to craft memories by finding activities you both enjoy and can do together.
****

A woman of a certain age knows what she wants and what she is about and is not likely to be easily pushed around or told what to do without voicing her strong option.

This can be a huge turn on for a man, but it can also be a cause for many arguments. If she has already bought her house and furnished it, she may want to keep it that way even when the man decides to move in and they are now living together.

The fact that she wears the pants in the relationship can sometimes work against her and she needs to know when to assert herself and when to hold back. Small things like this can drive wedges into a couple's union and need to be addressed at the onset of a relationship. Don't be afraid to assert yourself as the man in her life too.

Other lifestyle differences that are often overlooked are pastimes and hobbies. Depending with the age gap, you may find that with things even as simple as music there is a huge anomaly in your tastes. This isn't saying that you two cannot find common ground. A little patience and a little research into each other's preferences may surprise you as you discover music you are both inclined to.

Hobbies are also another area that can be a source of contention. A couple does not necessarily have to share every single activity together or be together all the time. In fact couples that spend time apart with other people and come together at the end of a day tend to be healthier. However it is a good idea to find activities that the two of you can equally engage in and enjoy as a couple. The key like with any relationship is to meet each other halfway and compromise.

Judgment From Society
Cultural norms that have existed for centuries will not suddenly disappear and change overnight. These norms can take as much as decades before people start accepting a new way of being.

Even though more and more women are now openly unafraid to be seen in public walking with their beaux, many of them still find it hard to go out in public except at night with their other halves. It is obvious to see how much society's footprint is still stamped heavily on people's consciences. It is a mental battle that cougars still have to overcome day in and day out.

Differing Commitment Levels
Women by nature once they have committed to a relationship like to throw themselves into the relationship wholeheartedly and they expect nothing less from their partner. This however, can be difficult, especially for a young man who is still full of life and is not really looking to be tied down and settle down.

Not every cougar is looking for marriage, but there are some that are, so if he is not looking to settle down just let it go and enjoy what you share for the time being. For cougars seeking to get married, being with a younger man who is not inclined in this way can be a heavy thing to bear for the both of you. Cubs, find out what she is about before you get any further.

Commitment and fidelity will both need to be addressed in the relationship to ensure that both parties are on the same page and are moving together in the same direction.

At times, older women who have been married before or who have been divorced may not be looking to remarry anytime soon, and may simply be looking for a man to be with for sexual reasons. Women still have needs too!

This is not saying that every unmarried older woman is not looking for love and remarriage, there are some women who are looking for both and at their age, they know they don't have time to waste so fortunately for you they won't beat about the bush much but will simply tell you what they want point blank and if you are moving in that direction then you can proceed, if not you can break of the relationship amicably.

Immaturity from the Man
A common misconception about men who date older women is that they have maternal issues; however this is not always the case because there are men who by nature are just attracted and drawn to older ladies. There is no shame in admitting that. However, women sometimes do find that some men can be a tad immature leading perhaps to people coming to the judgmental conclusion that their immaturity is because of mother issues.

Acting slightly immature can be a turn on for some women who can find it rather adorable at first, but continued immaturity can end up being a turn off and work against the man.

Immature things that men say that are tactless include saying things like, 'My, you have aged well,' or 'you look fantastic for your age.' If you are looking to stay alive don't say anything about her age – in fact don't even bring that subject up. Period.

When getting into a relationship with a younger man, the woman has accepted that the man is bound to act immature at some point because of his age, and she will give a certain leeway, take it but don't abuse it boys or it could be the end of you!

To say that every cougar is the same would be untrue. Every woman is different, but women who have chosen to embrace the cougar lifestyle have to face a lot of stereotypes that are thrown their way. When they start dating a younger man it is a misconception that is almost always prevalent that they are only after the intimacy. But, she is still a woman and she has other needs. So cubs, weigh these advantages that work against her and do your best to work on yourself so that she doesn't have to struggle with saying yes to you.

Chapter 4) Dating Advantages For The Male

The advantages of dating a woman who is older than you are unparalleled. Say goodbye to the headache of having to constantly be with an immature girl who doesn't know what she wants and say hello to a woman who is able to tell you *exactly* what she wants and *how* she likes it! Mature women don't waste your time beating about the bush; they are clear about what they want and are not ashamed to say it!

Life was never meant to be uptight and fret with little annoyances, and you are definitely going to appreciate that about Mrs Robinson because she lives her life with a relaxed attitude, she has gotten to that stage in life where she realises that she doesn't need to be limited by people's perceptions about her, she can just live as and how she pleases. *That* in itself is a liberating experience for anyone.

Dating an older woman is an experience that is riddled with so many exciting adventures for you as a younger man. You will grow in so many ways and learn new things that you never dreamed could be possible. Well, it comes with the territory of being in the company of one who has weathered life longer than you.

We are going to look at some of the key advantages for a cub when it comes to dating an older woman. Are you ready? Brace yourself, here they come:

Explosive Intimate Sex
Come on, you knew this was coming. She will rock your world in ways you have never imagined. If you thought sex could only be enjoyed in a few positions then prepare to be surprised. Get ready for the time of your life. You are guaranteed to learn a thing or two when you are with her. Let go and have fun. A woman of a certain age will have the tenacity to awaken things hidden in your heart that you have been too shy to confess to anyone else. She knows just how to make you lust after her and she knows exactly how to quench that insatiable desire deep within you. On the other end, it

is your duty to tell her she is beautiful, don't just be on the receiving end, and reciprocate the love. Romance her, and woo her and make her feel special. You want to bring her back to the days when men fell at her feet and chased her, make her feel that excitement all over again. Make her feel wanted and highly desirable.

Remember boys, no matter how experienced a woman may be, you get more honey with sweet words than you do with a sharp tongue. Tell her that *je ne sais quoi* and whisper those sweet nothings. She may laugh at the attempts but she will love you all the more for it. This, according to Joan Collins is the secret to her 14 year marriage to theatre executive Percy Gibsons who happens to be 32 years her junior.

No Strings Attached Fun
Older women know exactly what they want and they will let you know directly if they are looking to settle down or just enjoy a relationship with benefits.

Unlike dating younger women who 99% of the times are questioning indirectly on when you will pop the big question, older women are not enticed by such things. Given there are some older women who are seeking to get married, but it is not every older lady looking for a till death do us apart commitment.

Some older women are widows and are simply looking for a younger man to have fun with and keep them company, while some are divorced women and are **not** looking for long commitments just friendship with benefits.

Such single ladies are great fun to be with, they are playful and more relaxed in general which is a very attractive quality. After all, there is nothing quite as sexy as confidence in a woman and older women are generally a step ahead in this area than their younger compatriots.

Little Financial Pressure
The majority of older women are well established in their

respective careers and have no need of your money. They certainly don't need you to buy them anything, but a gesture here and there is always a lovely and thoughtful action which shows that you are still aware of her and want her to feel special.

However, we are going to mention here that if you ask her out, she is just like any woman and will expect you to foot the bill, perhaps for the first meal. In general though, if you ask her out on a date do NOT expect her to foot that the bill. That is just downright ill-mannered and is not gentlemanly at all. A slip up like that can cost you the relationship.

In this area of their life, older ladies have a certain sophistication and self-possession. They are clear about their finances and usually look after their own needs very well. If they bring you on board, they have taken into consideration where you are financially and whether or not you will be an asset or a liability to them. They are calculating like that. Don't underestimate their intelligence and their quick feminine intuition.

****

Gentlemen, just because she is financially sound and stable does not mean that you stop paying for the bill when you take her out for a date. She appreciates a man who shows that he can handle his own and take care of her as well.

More than anything an older woman is looking for a man who knows how to treat a lady. Don't mess around with this one because women are quick to dismiss men without manners.
****

As time goes on in your relationship you can always discuss and talk about the financial side of things because she will definitely be aware of the fact that perhaps your career is still just starting so she cannot expect you to buy her Cartier diamonds and take her out on a cruise around the world, but she will be expecting you to meet a certain threshold which is her own personal standard.

They Have MUCH To Teach You
An older woman knows just how to treat you in such a way as to

bring out that inner man in you. One of her goals may be to deliberately seduce you, but she also needs you to be her challenge. You need to give her a challenge, she lives for the thrill.

You will learn how to treat a woman; she will coach you unashamedly on what she expects and what is unacceptable in her eyes.

Etiquette and Manners

Be prepared to learn how to treat her well because she won't settle for anything less. You might as well start learning how to open car doors and how to hold doors open for ladies if you are not already doing so.

In a short amount of time you will find yourself knowing a whole lot more about women than before. If you want to keep her, you better treat her right because she knows her worth. You better treat her like the queen that she is.

Sitting down to dinner can be memorable events as you will be stimulated to intelligent conversation. Sometimes younger ladies can be a bore because their hearts and minds are clouded by thoughts and imaginations of starting families of their own, which for many mature women is no longer the case. Their interests are now varied and wide and thanks once again to their experience they have many more interesting topics to share and converse with you about.

Commitment

They will show you what commitment looks like and what it is. Mature women tend to be a whole lot more committed and stable, and they will expect the same from you.

Mrs Robinson is not your average Jill or Jane; she doesn't always need you and is not always up in your space like Jill will be. She is able and understands that as a man you need your space and will be able to give it to you without a grudge. Even with all this space she still remains devoted to you because she knows that a healthy relationship requires space, for two people to truly show their commitment to each other.

Health and Wellbeing

The older a woman gets, the more she values her own health and the more her efforts towards leading a healthier lifestyle increase. She is also aware of how to speak to you in such a manner as to encourage you to take care better care of yourself. Hence do not be surprised if you find yourself suddenly looking and feeling much better.

Higher Self-Esteem

The delightful Mrs Robinson knows exactly how to speak to you. She knows what you need to hear to bring out the best in you and can be quite unapologetic about pushing you to be your very best. Promotions in your job await you because of an increased self-confidence and self-esteem.

Knowing which battles to fight

When dating a younger woman the fights are almost always petty and immature which can be wearisome. Mrs Robinson knows that not every battle is worth bringing out the gloves for; experience has taught her that not every fight must be fought there are some fights not worth fighting. Her conflict resolution skills are more advanced and she is likely to be the first one to step in and diffuse a situation that could potentially get ugly.

Dating a mature woman should be an experience every man goes through because she will elevate you and bring out qualities in you that you never knew existed. She will encourage you to be the man you were born to be. As being with her and seeing how amazing she is and how envious others are of your relationship will make you want to be a better man to her.

Chapter 5) Dating Disadvantages For The Male

The battle of the mind and the negative thoughts that can plague a man about the relationship are one disadvantage a man has to learn to overcome.

It may be easy for a man to accept that his woman is older than him but it is something that the world at large may find unforgiving and will definitely remind him about every chance it gets. A cub has to reassure himself every day that it is perfectly okay to be with the woman he loves and wants.

The mind can be overcome and because of the lifestyle he has chosen, he will have to overcome it if he is to progress with loving his cougar lifestyle. Once this first hurdle is conquered, the man is better able to handle all the other challenges that may arise in his relationship with a cougar.

Male Stereotypes - The Need to First Break Stereotypes
For men the most common stereotypes and words that are thrown about are toy boy lovers and mama's boy.

These names imply men who grew up with maternal issues and are seeking an older woman to take the place of the mother they never had or to fulfil the role of a mother that their own mother may not have fulfilled as they were growing up.

Sadly this is a gross misrepresentation of these younger men. In the majority of cases, it is a deliberate act of free will on the part the man to go out with an older woman. There might be a handful of men with maternal issues, but 99% of them simply prefer older women.

In fact, after experiencing life with older women, a lot of these men find younger women simply boring and the levels of maturity really low. They discover that their interests have now become wider and they need more to stimulate them than the childish talk of younger maids. It's a bit like having tasted roast chicken, suddenly boiled chicken doesn't seem to be as tasty as it used to be.

Having to deal with this is one of the biggest challenges and disadvantages that men in relationships with older women have to endure. It shows society's double standards how you don't find older men who date younger women being labelled as harshly as men who decide to date older women.

Family Disapproval

Challenging societal norms will never be a walk in the park, especially when it comes time to introduce your partner to your family. It can be awkward if proper care is not taken with how you introduce your partner. Having your mother walk into your house and finding a woman almost her age dressed in your shirt with no pants is NOT the way to introduce your woman to your family.

Many times family members will always pick at something about the incoming in-law and with these kinds of relationships, despite all the other seemingly good qualities found in the woman, most people find it hard to look past her age. Is this the only challenge that faces males entering these kinds of relationships? Or there are other foreseeable disadvantages that need to weighed and considered?

Jealousy from Friends and Other Men

It is not uncommon to find that men who are older than you or your peers are not happy about your relationship with a mature woman. They may not voice it in words but it will be obvious to see the jealously on their part. Your friends may also find it socially awkward to continue hanging out with you and your lady, putting a strain on your relationship.

The Desire to Have Children and Start a Family

If an older woman already has her own children, then her mind, unlike that of a much younger woman, is not hell bent on having children. She may well be past that child bearing age with her focuses on other sights. She isn't looking at a man thinking 'will he make a good father and provider for my children?' If her children are young, it may be a thought that flashes across her mind but it will certainly not be the most dominant thought in her mind.

27

The desire to have children is a desire than many men have. One of the most common reasons for two people being together is that desire to start a family together. Men have the ability to keep having children until the day they die, but women are not designed like men. According to the normal course of life, women in general are able to have children from the time they hit their teenage year's right through to their thirties. It is rare for women to have children in their forties but it is not impossible.

Thanks to modern day advancements in medicine, women are able to have more control over their bodies and decide when and at what time they wish to have children. If a woman has not met the right man by the time she gets to thirty years of age, she can now make the decision to freeze her good eggs and keep them until she meets her Mr Right. When they desire to start a family they can simply unfreeze the eggs and mix them with the man's sperm and inject it into the woman's womb.

If a woman is still in her childbearing years and is unable to have children and the man wants children, then the couple can consider having a surrogate mother step in and give birth to their child.
****
The numbers of people who consider adoption on a yearly basis are more than 2 million, and this is a combination of both fertile and infertile couples. Keep your options open if you would like to start a family.
****
Another option that is increasingly becoming popular is that of adoption. If as a man you desire to have a family and your partner is past her childbearing age, then adoption is a likely path that can be considered.

Children from Previous Marriage (s)
If a woman has children from a previous marriage then this is something that you must take into consideration, especially if you wish to take this relationship forward to the next level. Children can feel resentment and fail to understand the choice their mother is making especially, if they themselves are of an age that is closer to their mother's lover. Regardless of the children's age, disclosing

their relationship to the children is the first step to welcoming the man into the family and should be approached with great care and timing is of great importance.

Lifestyle Choices
An older woman knows exactly what she wants and may be set in her ways and trying to get her to change is like trying to change the course of a river. This is not saying it's not possible but it will be extremely difficult. As people get older they tend to become set in their ways as they become comfortable with who they are.

This will contrast with your potential lifestyle as you are still young and enjoying all that life has to offer, and perhaps you are still finding out just what you like and what you don't like in life. This area seems petty but can be a real tough one, especially when two people decide to move in together.

Differing Wants and Needs
In her younger days a woman may want to feel loved and made to feel pretty and attractive because she is in her youth and at that stage where she believes her looks are what is most important. However, an older woman's needs may have shifted and now she is focussed on security and is more concerned with being secure in life. She now knows that beauty fades and life will take its toll on her looks and figure so she is less concerned about them, but she does enjoy it when you flatter her and compliment her sincerely.

All these disadvantages warranty careful thought, but you don't have to wait to have it all figured out before you make a move on a cougar. You can work through these issues together as they arise.

Younger men and older women couplings are just like any other relationship and they face challenges that are similar to any other relationship. Yes there may be a few dynamics that are different and need to be addressed but so long as both parties are happy and fully committed to the relationship and willing to make it work then there is nothing that cannot be overcome by the two of them.

At Work
So you thought you were the only one with the hots for your lady

boss, but it turns out you are not the only one. Lots of cubs have admitted that they fancy their bosses and think about them inappropriately sometimes without even realizing it.

Fortunately for you, she may even have reciprocal feelings but she tries to keep it strictly professional. Don't pursue her in the workplace; that would be unprofessional, seek her outside the work scenario. You will be surprised by the mutual feeling that can develop. Don't stalk her because no one likes a stalker, not even a cougar.

If you are definitely sure that she is into you, before you make a move that may be ill calculated, do something spontaneous like send her an anonymous bouquet of flowers. Don't sign your name obviously but if you want you can put in your initials or keep her guessing.

If you see her responding and taking the bait then you can gradually reveal yourself to her with time.

If you are not the patient kind of guy, then you can do the daring thing and wait for her by her car or slip her a note with your name and phone number. Just be sure though about your suspicions, if you think she digs you then you better confirm it somehow because the last thing you want is a call from HR telling you that you have a red tag with sexual harassment on your profile for having made inappropriate remarks to your female superior.

Supermarkets
You were pushing your grocery cart and she was coming your way and didn't see you. The next thing you know you both crash into each other. You both laughed to diffuse the situation and got up apologizing frenetically, then you looked into her eyes, and she looked into yours and well, it was love at first sight. As corny as it sounds, it does happen to a sufficient number of men, a whopping 5% to be precise. Fine, it may not happen in *that* exact manner, but supermarket bumps-ins have sometimes led to the best cougar/cub encounters and hook-ups for some lucky individuals.

Perhaps your eyes met across the shelves, or she was trying to grab something off the top shelf and you stepped in to help her, whichever way it happened, the point is it could happen to you, so keep your eyes open the next time you are at the supermarket.

Gym

We all know her, the hot blonde or brunette with great legs, hair pulled in a tight pony tail, abs that look like you could eat off of them and well, the body of a goddess. She usually walks around with her earphones plugged in so you barely ever manage to say hi, but when you do, she is the kind of woman that when she flashes you a smile, it is the most beautiful smile you have ever seen. It literally knocks the air out of your sails and you have to pinch yourself and bring yourself back to Earth.

Yes her. We are talking about her, but the thing is you didn't know she was older than you when you hit on her and then she surprised you and accepted your advances. But who cares, age is just a number right? Well a good percentage of cubs believe so, and we couldn't agree more!

Your Mother's Friend / Your Best Friend's Mother

Oh boy, this one takes the trophy. This situation places you dead center in the awkward and uncomfortable zone where you are literally walking on eggshells around your mother and whenever you go to your best friend's house.

It has probably got to be the one time that cubs find it hard to say no, although they really, really want to hook up with her. Why does life have to be so complicated? When these types of cougar/cubs relationships happen, let's just say they don't really go past the, 'let's be friends with benefits zone'. It kind of starts and ends here. Looking for more would be asking for trouble.

If you are prepared to ruin your relationship with your mother for life and betray the trust of your best friend, then you can go ahead, but if for goodness' sake you have a conscience, break it off before it goes any further. If not for yourself, then do it for your mother's sake.

Bars and Clubs

Bars and clubs traditionally used to be the most common dating minefields. Today bars and nightclubs have fallen in second place as the most successful route used by men to meet and find cougars to date. Believe it or not, but there are cities where cougar events are actually held and people attend and enjoy themselves and meet new people, and for those lucky in love, find their perfect cougar/cub!

Probably for the first time ever, the average age that most women are when they finally decide to settle down and get married is 29.9 years. Yes that's almost 30! As you are enjoying yourself in the bar and club, you never know who you are dancing with or really just how old (or young) the girl is. It's not uncommon nowadays to find women in their 30's still hanging around bars. What makes it harder to distinguish their age is also the fact that they are smoking hot.

Cougars trawling these bars are not your ordinary kind of woman. These women take real good care of themselves and sometimes even look younger than the young girls. It has been the experience of many guys after several dates to finally find out their date is in fact older than they are. But by that time, the spark is already there and Cupid's arrow has hit both hearts.

This is great for those, whose social skills are able to carry them with grace, but what if you are a young man who really wants to hook up with a cougar but you just don't know how to express yourself to her in person?

The Online Dating Scene

Fortunately for you who may be a bit shy and find it hard to express yourself well in person, or are too busy to go clubbing, there are several online platforms that you are able to take advantage of and connect with different women from literally all over the world.

This is the best and most successful way to meet cougars, this is according to a survey on cubs done by Cougared founder Oliver

Jameson in 2011. Nearly 5 out of every 10 men said this was by far their best option when it came to meeting cougars.

All it takes is a simple registration process which includes filling in your profile and adding a few attractive pictures here and there, making connections and waiting for an invitation from someone – or if you are the adventurous one, be the first to introduce yourself and get to know the other person.

The advantage of online dating services is that one can dictate the pace of the relationship and you don't have to meet someone in person until you are both ready.

You also don't have to go through the pain of rejection in person. Furthermore, you can initiate conversation with as many people as you like at any given time. You get to avoid all the nervous jitters you get if you had to muster the courage to walk up to someone in a bar.

Matchmaker profiles are also a great way to find partners you are highly compatible with and this can be tailored to find people who live in your area or country. There are tools to help you get started that are not necessarily available in the real world dating game. To be honest, online dating can be really fun for those who find it hard to meet people in typical social settings.
****

The information from the websites listed below was correct at the time of printing. However, the internet changes rapidly so some websites might change their conditions or some websites may no longer exist when you are reading this book.
****

For those who really don't have a clue where to begin below we list some of the hottest and best social media platforms for finding younger men/older women online.

COUGAR LIFE www.cougarlife.com

Advantages
Women join free so there are lots of women to connect with
Limited number of free messages at the start

Associated fees
Monthly cost of $29 / £18.50
When your messages run out you have to purchase what are known
as credits (100 credits for $10 / £6.39)

****

*The idea for Cougar Life was birthed out of Claudia Opdenkelder's
own life experience. She says of herself, 'I had many friends who
would come up to me and ask me where was I finding all these
handsome men?'*
*These questions set the ball rolling for Claudia and put her out on
the path to creating the world's premier cougar dating website in
2009.*

****

Cougar Life is one of the premier sites that have been around for
more than five years. It was started in 2009 by Claudia
Opdenkelder. The smoking hot cougar bombshell was only 39 at
the time but was living with her then 25 year old boyfriend.
Within its first 9 months, Cougar Life had more than 200,000
subscribers; today they have one of the largest member databases
among the top cougar dating websites with over 850,000 monthly
visitors.

Today Cougar Life is the biggest and arguably the most well-
known cougar dating platform on the planet.

- **So what sets Cougar Life apart from the rest?**

Cougar Life has an active and large scale marketing and
advertising campaign that sees many new subscriptions being
logged in daily by the hundreds. Television commercials and
internet ads, Cougar Life does it all. This is something that other
websites fail to do, and hence lose potential customers.

Cougar Life, because of its head start advantage and great advertising, has the largest active database of all the cougar dating websites around and this is what is most important in any dating service, you just simply have to have people in order for the website to go on.

The men to women ratio on the website is 2 men to every woman, so the chances of being paired up with someone are half and half which is ideally not bad at all. It is better to have the hope of being able to find someone than going to a bar where you really don't know what the odds will be. There are 850,000 monthly visitors of which 62% are men and 38% are women.

So how does the website work, can you join for free or there are terms and conditions to look into?
Cougar Life gives you a free trial period, so you can actually test all the features and even make great connections with members before the trial period ends.

This is really a neat option as it allows you the chance to fully evaluate and see whether it will be worth investing money into month after month. If you are happy with the service that is offered on the website, once your trial period has expired you will be required to pay a monthly subscription fee to enable you to continue accessing all the unique features available to active members on the website.

The monthly charges will be automatically deducted from the PayPal account you registered with or your credit card. The PayPal charges can be spotted easily and cancelled if you don't want to continue but the credit card charges can be a pain, so if you do end up registering on this site, ensure that you use your PayPal account so that you can track your monthly fees.

Things to consider
Don't make your profile brief. Keep it interesting enough that a cougar will be able to read a bit about you and know what they are getting into when they start chatting to you.

You will need a valid credit card to verify your age.

COUGARED www.cougared.com

Advantages
Free signup, takes less than a minute
Free member benefits:
Allow you to add up to 27 photos, interact with subscribed members, see latest activities from members, read cougar profiles and see date ideas.
There are tools that will match you up and allow you to search for cougars by age, body type, new members, children, location and even the kind of relationship they are after!

Associated fees
Free membership for standard members
Gold membership
1 month $29.95 / £19.14
3 months $59.95 / £38.32 (this is about $19.95/ £12.75 per month)
6 months $99.95 / £63.89 (this is about $16.66 / £10.65 per month)

Cougared was founded by bold and proud cub Oliver Jameson and in 2011 in response to a survey that piqued his interest. Jameson ran a survey among cubs in a bid to understand just what happens in the mind of a cub and what they really think about cougars and the entire cougar-cub dating world. Common questions that Jameson and his team at Cougared wanted to find out included:

- Do you date older women just for the sex or there are other reasons?
- Do you have a celebrity fantasy crush that you would like to get cougared by?
- Do you think cougars should retire, if yes, at what age?
- Have you ever been in an awkward position where you found your mother's best friend making advances towards you and behaving inappropriately?

And....Meet the parents...
- What was your parents' reaction when they found out about your cougar crush?

Equipped with the answers to this survey, Jameson and his team built an even stronger website that is geared and aimed at young men like you. The website offers real life advice from those who have been in the game longer and those who know exactly what to expect from a cougar/cub relationship.

So if you are clueless and are looking for more help as to what to do and what steps to take, then be sure to check out Couagered.com.

While most sites require you to pay after their free initial trial period has expired, Cougared is in a class of its own and requires no such sign-up or follow- up fees. It is simply a matter of signing up and well, getting your game face on and having fun.

What makes Cougared a great website for both cougars and cubs?
Come on, who doesn't like free things on this planet? We all enjoy free goodies, and well, the chance to hook up with a hot cougar at no extra cost is a great deal for any cub.

Monthly charges for different sites can get quite costly very fast, with Cougar Life being a prime example that charges up to $29 (£18.54) per month in subscription fees.

Fortunately with Cougared, there are no hidden costs, what you see is what you get.

Cougared fees and payment options

If you want to get premium access to the site then you have to upgrade your free membership to that of a gold member. When you become a gold member you are able to increase your chances of meeting the right cougar by as much as 500%. Your profile has the ability to be seen via mobile phones, which raises the chances of you being contacted by at least 20 times. You will also be able to access your messages faster. The gold membership plan is available for consideration when you are ready to upgrade.

Payments may be made using your credit / debit card or your charge and check cards, money order, pay pal account.

DATE A COUGAR www.dateacougar.com

Advantages
Signing up is free and so is searching

Dateacougar associated fees
Subscription fees begin at $13.33 per month / £8.52 per month

Dateacougar is owned and run by Elite Marketing Solutions Inc. that was founded in 2006.

Dateacougar is an awesome site for those who are sticklers for detail. The profiles on this site are quite lengthy as their unique selling proposition is trying to match people based on common interests. This can be a great option for those who don't have the time to sit down and go through a cougar's profiles personally. They can simply sit back and let the system's matchmaker do all the hard work for them while they enjoy the whole process.

To date this is still a relatively small and intimate group of people, hence finding your match here is highly likely as there are only less than a 1000 members.

The one aspect about this website that we didn't quite understand is why they allow younger women onto the site when it is clearly a cougar website.

The other things to know about dateacougar.com are that you can sign up for free but once you have activated your membership, the fees start from $13.33 / £8.52 per month.

When you are accessing the site, you will be allowed to send messages as well as ask if she is interested. You can also send flirts as well as do IM chatting.

COUGAR DATES www.cougardates.com

Advantages
Free sign up and register allows you to access to a profile where
you can add up to 26 photos.
Search cougars by city and country
Build a list of favorite cougars
Send an unlimited number of winks

Associated fees and benefits:
Cost per month: $70 / £44.74
Upgrade yourself to the status of a gold member and you are
entitled to the following:
Chat online and send emails without limitation
You have greater control over photo and profile security options
You can use the compatible matches tool
You can see the last time someone was online
You can use the advanced search for people tool

This website is probably the fastest and easiest to register with – it
takes less than a minute to register. The home page is also
relatively uncluttered, allowing the opportunity to navigate the site
easily and get around without too much complication.

TOYBOY www.toyboy.com

Advantages
Initial membership is free

Associated fees
Monthly full membership begins at £19.95 / $31.21 per month

This UK born site is one of the premier cougar/cub dating sites
around. This site is one of the few sites we have seen that actually
has a really great design. Although it is geared and aiming at older
and mature women and cubs, this site focuses less on the dating
aspect of the game and centers more on building a community
among the members of the group. I guess this is okay if you are
looking for something slow where you allow yourself time to get to

know people and build friendships.

Within this community you can send video chats, people keep diaries, some have video profiles, and you can instant message and even send virtual gifts. It's more of a mature social networking site if you ask us.

Something we have against this website is the important issue of age restriction. Women between the ages of 18-30 shouldn't really be considered in the cougar category and hence, should not be allowed on this kind of site.

Creating a profile on bemytoyboy.com is free, but in order to become a full member, you will be required to pay a monthly £19.95 ($31.21) subscription fee.

URBAN COUGAR www.urbancougar.com

Come on, the name gives it away. This platform is filled with premier cougars and not just your ordinary kind of cougar. Think Sex and the City or Desperate Housewives. We are talking about sophisticated women here.

The cougars on this website are not looking for random hookups. They are looking for a little bit more; they want committed, no strings attached relationships and well, friends with benefits. If this is what you are after with a cougar, then don't hesitate to join Urban Cougar today.

COUGARS MEET www.cougarsmeet.com

Online dating can be a really good option to those who don't have time to go onto the regular dating social scenes. In fact, in a survey conducted by Oliver Jameson of Cougared in 2011, it was discovered that 49% of cubs found their cougar mates online.

Cougarsmeet.com is a really unique platform that gives you the ability to truly meet up and get to know cougars from all walks of life. The site offers a range of features that are uncommon on other sites. It is these features that set this website apart from the rest and increase your chances of meeting up with the right cougar.

COUGAR FLING **www.cougarfling.com**

Advantages
Easy set up and free standard sign up
Most members come from the USA

Associated costs
Premium membership
$7.95 / £5.08 for a 3 day trial
$29.95 / £19.14 per month
$39.99 / £25.56 for 3 months ($13.33 / £8.52 every month)

Payment options
Credit cards – Visa and MasterCard
eCheck

Rich older women looking for hot younger men to spoil and lavish is the name of the game on this website. The hot mamas on this website aren't looking for long term relationships. They are looking to have fun. If this is what you are after, look no further because Cougar Fling is here to meet your needs.

11% of cubs interviewed by Oliver Jameson, founder of Cougared, admitted that they were looking for a rich hot mama to spoil them.

The user interface of the website is really easy to use and navigate. The greatest advantage cougars have on this website is the large numbers of men who outnumber them on the site. It really is a place where you have to put your best foot forward because the competition for cougar attention is stiff.

For those who are lucky enough to hook up with a hot cougar via this platform, they are in for a really stupendous time.

BE COUGAR www.becougar.com

Advantages
Limited access to chat rooms, profiles, search tools

Associated costs
6 month package costs a little over $10 / £6.39 per month

Although this website has one of the larger membership databases (over 1 million subscribers of any of the cougar dating sites) it remains one of the less popular sites. However it is still a great entry level platform for any newbie cougars or cubs. It's a great place to interact and learn the ins and outs of online dating.

COUGAR911 www.cougar911.com

Advantages
Live chat with local members
Free trial

Associated costs
Subscription fee $50 / £31.96

If you are a cougar or cub raring to go and need to find a mate as soon as possible, then this is the website for you.

This is probably the number one no-strings-attached website to get yourself hooked onto. This site is just downright the best when it comes to its free trial period. You have just got to get yourself registered onto this site to learn more about its amazing offers. We are sure that once you enter Cougar911, you will never want to leave.

Think of it as your own personal 911 service for getting in touch with local cougars.

PLAYCOUGAR www.playcougar.com

Advantages
Free signup at the start
Women send chat messages free of charge

Associated costs
Subscriptions for paying members are £7.99 / $12.50 per month

Explicit is the name of the game on playcougar.com. If you are seriously looking for hook-ups without too much hassle, then this is the site for you. The number of active members upon last count was under 50,000 according the latest dating reviews. The signup process is pretty straightforward. After you have signed up, you can proceed to create a profile without difficulty.

A paying member can access a host of features such as sending more than one icebreaker to a woman. You will be able to continue messaging, text chatting and video chatting as well.

A useful feature that is available on the site is that of being able to mark clearly whether or not you are available the next day for a meet-up.

Things to note about playcougar.com are the price per month which is £7.99 / $12, 50 and also the fact that you should never open this site at work or where children are present because of the sexually explicit nature of the ads that pop up on the top and bottom of the site. You have been warned!

TOYBOYWAREHOUSE www.toyboywarehouse.com

Advantages
Free signup at the onset of your journey on toyboywarehouse
Guaranteed real people to connect with, no ghost profiles
Free members may search and flirt, send winks; have favourites and send cards.

Associated costs

Upgrading to premium member will cost you £12.49 ($19.54) per month.

But it allows you unrestricted access to the entire site and all features such as who 'favoured' your profile, who viewed your profile and so forth.

We hope that at least by now you are aware that each website offers its own perks and disadvantages. There are websites for those strictly looking for rich hot cougars to have a good time with, and there are websites for those who are just simply out to make 'friends' and network, and then there are sites where hook-ups are for friends with benefits.

Now if you are looking for a friends-with-benefits website, then this website, toyboywarehouse.com, is not for you.

The cougars on this website are the passive aggressive cougars defined in Chapter One. These cougars are here for the long term ride. We are talking about divorcees, widows, and single women who are looking for more than just a random hook-up. If this is the kind of cougar that you are after, then by all means feel free to sign up as soon as possible!

Toyboywarehouse.com began in 2006 when proud owner and founder of the website Julia Macmillan, who has always felt attracted and intrigued by younger men, realized that she was not the only woman who was into younger men.

She is quoted on the website saying that the topic of older women who were into younger men was a topic that was often discussed hush, hush behind closed doors because of its taboo nature.

But the moment she realized that she was not alone in her love for young men, and seeing that there was no website available for younger men and mature women to mix and mingle freely on social platforms, the idea for toyboywarehouse was birthed. Years later the site proudly states that a lot of the relationships that were started on this platform continue to grow and thrive with some couples even having gone ahead to settle down and have children! Today the website boasts a modest yet sizeable 20,000 members.

So, how do you go about registering yourself onto this amazing site? At the beginning of your membership on toyboywarehouse.com, you don't have to pay anything, it is free to join. You only start paying for your membership when you upgrade your membership and the cost is £12.49 per month ($19.54 per month).

The great thing about this site is that unlike other websites, it does not hide costs from you. Everything is written in black and white and you can read it for yourself.

A big plus we give this website is the fact that the membership is not an automated experience. Every month once your membership expires, the site automatically downgrades you back to a free member and it will be up to you whether you would like to renew your membership or keep it as a free account.

With a free account you will be allowed to use features such as sending winks and cards and you can even search the website's database. Great interactions and tools on the site include forums and events that make life really simple for someone who would like to meet people in the flesh in a group environment.

Toyboywarehouse also likes putting in that personal touch when it comes to profiles. There have been cougar dating websites which have been accused of creating fake profiles to give the illusion of there being more members than actually exist. These 'ghost' members per se are automated accounts that are run and monitored by the powers that are behind the websites.

Toyboywarehouse however prides itself on being one of the very few websites that do not use this deceptive method, and who manually add and approve every application that is lodged. There is an in-house team that does nothing but make sure that every profile that is created meets the website's standards to ensure only the best quality for the active members on the site.

COUGAR LOVER www.cougarlover.co.uk

Advantages
Free sign up
Basic membership allows you to send winks and receive alerts

Associated Costs
Premium membership
£24.95 per month ($39.60)
£79.95 for 6 months (£16.65 per month) ($79.29 for 3 months / $26.43 per month)
£124.95 for 1 year (£10.42 per month) ($198.33 per month / $16.54 per month)

Payment options
Credit cards – visa and MasterCard
SMS mobile payment

This site is geared for the UK market helping the sexy cougars here hook up with younger men. The user interface on this website is relatively simple. The basic features on this site are pretty much like those on every other dating site. You will have your free tools and messages before you have to upgrade your membership.

One of the biggest let-downs on this website is the inability to chat online. Online chatting is basic so we don't know how they could have neglected this all important part of developing their website.

The current female membership base of this website stands at 454,669 cougars waiting to be reached. Profiles contain the location, interests, what the cougar is looking for and photos amid other cool features.

GO COUGAR www.gocougar.com

Advantages
Detailed profiles
Guest book feature allows you to leave comments
Send winks as ice breakers
IM feature allow you instant chatting
Ability to favourite as well available

Associated costs
Free for standard members
Upgrading to Pro membership will cost you:
$9.95 per month (£6.36)
$25.95 for 3 months (£16.59)
$49.95 for 6 months (£31.93)

Payment options
Credit card – Visa, MasterCard, American Express, Discover
PayPal, Bank transfer

The reach of this platform is global and doesn't focus or concentrate on only one geographical area. A bonus that we liked and appreciated on this website was their reductions in subscription fees. Perhaps this is due partly to how difficult the site is to use?

This site has its positives and its drawbacks. If you are into vintage and old fashioned settings then you might like the way the website is structured, if not then you will hate it.

The majority of the members on this website flood in from the US, Europe and Canada. The latest statistics suggest that there are less than 10, 000 female subscriptions.

If you want to find people quickly there are general search options available. To help you meet up with active members, you can see the last time someone was active on the site so that you don't waste time sending messages to inactive members.

Another fantastic feature we liked was 'My Matches' which

attempts to pair you up with people the system thinks will be your best match. This is done based on the profiles of cougars you have visited.

Blogs give you the chance to read what other people are saying and can also be a great way for people to know what you are up to if you do decide to keep an online journal yourself.

OLDER WOMEN DATING www.olderwomendating.com

Advantages
Free registration and profile creation
Large active member base
Great features which are easy to use
Great user interface
Affordable pricing

Associated fees
Upgrade to gold membership
$21.95 per month (£14.03)
$59.95 for 3 months (£38.32)
$95.95 for 6 months (£61.33)

Payment options
Credit card – Visa, MasterCard, America Express, PayPal, Personal check or money order

Favoured by some as being the premier cougar dating site even above common leader Cougar Life, Older Women Dating is said to be in a league of its own for the following reasons.

It is tasteful; the website's features are fun and easy to use, the glossy finish of the site and large active membership base are attractive features on any website. All this is combined with very competitive subscription rates that are too good to be true for the service that is delivered.

In a nutshell, this website contains everything you could want to make sure that you find yourself a cougar. If ever there was a website you should join, it is this one right here.

Every relationship option is represented here, whether you are looking for some dating fun or just a casual friendship or indeed a long term commitment, you can find it all here at Older Women Dating. With a member base that exceeds one million, the chances of you meeting the right cougar for you are extremely enormous.

The detailed profiles of members gives you the chance to really get to know people before you start sending them messages and in this way they can read up on you as well before they respond. This helps you both hit the ground running and start a genuine conversation, which can be the start of a good relationship.

Email is the method of communication that is standard and like on other sites the easiest way to break the ice is to send a wink. The only disappointment we encountered on the website was the lack of chat rooms.

Older Women Dating has the largest forum and blog features of any cougar dating community or website.

IMPORTANT WEBSITE DATING TIPS FOR CUBS

In order to get the best results from online dating sites, the following hot tips will make sure you keep your head in the game and have your best foot forward.

Top Tip No.1 Read Her Profile – All of it!
Guys don't skip out on the details, don't think you can get away with not reading her profile, you will get caught and she will not be impressed. It is a little investment for what awaits you in the future if you play your cards right. So stop going through her pictures only and start taking time to read what she has written about herself.

Top Tip No.2 Chat as often as you can on the platform first
You may be tempted to take things to the next level and you may think you should ask her for her phone number, email or other

means of communication.

On this one we say hold your horses Johnny boy, first make sure you have established a good connection on this dating platform before you run off into swapping numbers and emails.

Top Tip No. 3 take 'no' graciously
There are some cubs out there who sadly don't know how to take 'no' for an answer with grace. A woman will learn a lot about your character by how you handle rejection. If you retaliate with insults and worse, then you can kiss goodbye to her ever coming back again. However, a self-possessed goodbye can get her thinking and even come back to you again, so don't rob yourself of a potential comeback.

Top Tip No.4 Never upload naked photos of yourself
As tempted as you may be to show her how manly you are and how gifted you are in certain departments, NEVER upload a naked photo of yourself to your chat platform.

This includes pictures of your manhood even if your face is not showing, it's just in poor taste and is not likely to impress the cougar you are after. So DON'T do it. If she wants to see more she will tell you, if no, don't do it no matter how tempted you are.

Top Tip No.5 Your profile picture is your first point of contact
Cubs, listen. She doesn't care about your car, your bike, your group of friends and definitely not your ex, so don't put up photos of these things. If you put up a group photo, how is she meant to find you among those faces? And why would you be putting up a picture of yourself with your ex? And if you have kids, you and your adorable family pictures are not to be uploaded, no matter how cute your child is. To a cougar it's just a nonstarter boys, don't do it.

Top Tip No.6 Personalize every message, cougars do notice
Cougars notice everything about your messages, from your tone of voice to your choice of words, to how appropriate they are to her, and if not she can tell whether this is just a bulk message you send

to all the women on your potential list of cougars. This is a big no, no.

Take the time to write a personal message, include something you read in her profile to show her that the message is indeed for her. Listen cubs, if you don't have the time to sit down and write a message to her, then you have no business going after her. A cougar wants to be treated like a queen, like she is the only woman you have your eyes set upon. So she will see through your bulk message a mile away and discard you and throw you in the trash if you are not careful.

Top Tip No.7 don't put your personal contact details into the very first message

Not only does doing this say you see her as a booty call, but it can be taken as being very rude. It shows you are neither considerate nor interested in her, only yourself.

While some women might respond, the majority of women will ignore you and block you from ever contacting them again, and we are sure this is not what you want. So on your first chat with her or your first message to her, keep it simple. Flirt, compliment her, flirt a bit more and let her bite the bait you have laid.

Top Tip No.8 The First Message

HI MY NAME IS SIMON. DO YOU WANNA CHAT? Sounds like you are shouting and screaming for her attention. Three words – major turn off. Let the capital letters do their job. Use them at the beginning of a sentence or when writing a name and keep it at that.

Capital letters in your conversation make it look like you are shouting, so stay clear of them. The other thing to keep in mind about your first message – avoid making it too lengthy. This is not a biography of your life. Leave the details to your profile. Your first message should be you trying to strike up a conversation and not boring her to death with your life story, she will have plenty of time to hear it one day.

Top Tip No. 9 Never introduce intimate talk into your chats
This one is a biggie especially when you haven't even been
intimate with her yet and even after the two of you have been
intimate; do not put your explicit experiences down in chat unless
she is okay with it. Ask her first if she is fine with it, if not then
stay away from it.

*Please note I have not personally used all of these websites listed
above. Before you become a member of these sites, make sure you
read their terms and conditions of use. Understand the membership
fees and how they are paid before entering bank card details and
attaching your account to these websites.

Please be aware that there are also many scam websites that exist
for the sole purpose of defrauding you of your money and in some
cases, stealing your personal information.

If you make arrangements to meet with someone you have met
online, make arrangements to meet in a public place. Human
trafficking is a real issue.

Chapter 6) How Would You Attract A Cougar/Younger Male?

Cubs, if you have your eyes set on the hottest woman around, who just so happens to be a tad bit older than you, then you will have to up your skills game. Your Jill and Jane games are not going to woo her and win her heart. You are going to have to put in a little more effort than that. Below we tell you just how to subtly attract a cougar, tame her and keep her!

Does she see you in the first place?!
There is a difference between her being able to see you and her noticing you. Let's start from there. A woman can see a man and well, that's just it, she sees you but the thought of the two of you being together may never cross her mind. That's the thing boys, you need to make her notice you, so how will you make her take notice of you?
Start in the small things.

- **Good Manners**

Manners, a man with impeccable manners stands out immediately in this world where good manners seem to have gone down a global drain. Holding her door as she enters or leaves a room, politely asking how she is doing and maintaining eye contact with her as she replies will instantly make her take notice of you. Women are attuned to these small antics and no matter how strong and independent a woman becomes she will always appreciate a well-mannered man.

So now that you have her attention, we come to the second part, what she sees.

- **Grooming**

Gentlemen, no cougar is ever going to give you a second glance if you are unkempt and look like you don't know when the last time you had a bath was. Keep your hair trim and neat, if you prefer to have it long learn how to maintain it well. Clothes must be ironed properly boys. She doesn't want to look like she is hanging onto the arm of a teenager still living out of his parent's garage. That is a major turn off cubs.

- **Touch**

Women are sensitive sensual creatures who respond to touch. Touching her elbow or her shoulder can be indicators to her that you like her without her feeling threatened. Don't overstep your boundaries. Take your cues from her.

- **Smile**

And lastly, nothing beats a handsome smile. Smile, it says hello in more ways than one. If you are comfortable enough, lean in and give her a kiss on the cheek, just make sure that if you do this, use great cologne that is not too heavy and will complement that manly smell. You want her to see you for the man that you are and not some boy with just a girly crush on her. Remember, smile and maintain eye contact, nothing is sexier than that.

These tips will help you get noticed by her. So now that she notices you, what next?

Understand who she is before you...open your mouth

A cougar isn't a pussy cat. She knows what she is about. She is confident, sassy and can be a bit of a flirt but she is no walk over. She isn't going to be easily impressed by childish flirting although she can play along.

Okay so you notice her sitting at the bar table, looking every bit as confident as any woman can, and darn sexy. You are looking presentable and have done everything right up till this stage. You gathered enough courage to go up and introduce yourself, you smiled and even touched her elbow and volunteered to buy her a drink. She looks impressed and invites you to take the seat next to her.

Then she asks,
'So, you are into banking, what do you think about the economic recession and its implications on the future of the world?' She

might as well have punched you in the stomach because your mind has suddenly gone blank. You stammer and stutter, well the truth is you do work in a bank, but you have never really been interested in all that, you just do the job because you have to. Well you kind of begin to start hating yourself in that moment as you see her face change from interest to annoyance in a matter of seconds.

So, let's rewind the scenario, *this* is what you should have done.

Read widely
An older woman is interested in a world other than her own. Her interests are vast and wide and will expect you to be at least educated and informed as to the current issues being discussed on the news and newspapers. You don't have to know and understand the laws of quantum physics, but knowing the headlines of what is happening in the world at large and having your own opinions demonstrates to her that you actually have a brain and it works!

Remember she doesn't have to be with you. Why should she stay with you? If you want her then you are going to have to pursue her until you get her and if that means raising your general knowledge then so be it. She is worth it and she knows it.

The first meeting has gone well, she is impressed and you can see it. Now should you ask her for her phone number or give her yours?

- **Exchanging Numbers**
To be honest, you may not get a second chance with her if you don't ask for her number. But how do you ask her for her number?

Don't be casual about it. Thank her sincerely for the evening and express your desire to see her again. If she mentioned something during your conversation about things she enjoys doing, you better have been listening.

Perhaps she mentioned loving art work, you could start the exchanging of details conversation a little like this, 'Rosemary, I have thoroughly enjoyed spending time with you this evening. On

Friday, the Art Museum is open until 7pm, how about I take you there and you can show me all the amazing artwork by the artists you spoke about this evening? Can I pick you up around 6.30pm?'

Not only does this show that you enjoyed her company and would like to see her again, but it also shows that you were paying attention to what she was saying and even processed it enough to think of a special place to take her. Of course if you have to pick her up, she must now give you her phone number so you can call and check up on her. Game set match!

Chapter 7) Keeping a Cougar/Younger Male Interested

Congratulations on winning her over, but the journey is just beginning and life is just about to get more fun so brace up!

A hot, smart and confident woman is sure to get a lot of passes from a lot of men, both younger than her and older than her. Don't think you are the first and the last to make a pass at her.

Don't build on a lie

Mrs Robinson may have said yes to your advances but that doesn't mean that she is completely yours now. You still have to maintain what you obtained. You cannot stop being a gentleman now. If you won her over by opening her car door and pulling up her chair for her, then you are going to have to continue doing that in order to keep her. If you bought her flowers and she loved them, then put a weekly reminder to get her flowers.

Affirm her

Cougars, despite what many people think, are still women. They still share the same insecurities as younger women and sometimes their insecurities may be more, although you may not get to see these insecurities as much as you would when you are with a younger woman.

A cougar needs you to affirm her and make her feel like she is the only one is the world that you have your eyes and affections set on. She is a queen and she expects to be treated as such. She knows her worth and understands very clearly that she can easily walk away if she is not being treated with the respect and courtesy that she deserves.

So if you want to keep her, and keep her happy, you will need to continue with these affirmations.

She is not your home girl

While older men may find it amusing and see nothing wrong with paying for their younger girl friend's needs, the reverse is not true. A cougar is not prone to paying your bills for you. She is not your ticket to a better life and she can spot a leech a mile away. Even though she has the money she wants you to prove to her that you are man enough to take care of your own business.

Under no circumstance will she allow herself to be called or referred to as a 'sugar mama' and you should stay away from any situations that would require her to help you financially e.g. getting locked up and asking her to come and post your bail, or failing to pay your own rent. Such things are major turn offs for any woman, so make sure you have your own financial life in order.

This doesn't mean you must be a millionaire before you can ask her out for more dates, but it simply means she should be able to see that you are responsible when it comes to matters of finance.

Work on your self-confidence

Nothing puts off a cougar than a wimp or a man who cannot stand up for himself. Women by nature are drawn to strong characters who exhibit leadership traits. She needs a man who can challenge her and rise up to the occasion of being in charge, not a coward who hides behind her whenever a problem or a situation arises.

Insecurity is unattractive and so is having stalker-like tendencies. Her world does not revolve around you, she was okay before you came and is likely to be just fine after you leave so never assume that she is more invested in you than you are into her. Keep her on the edge by being confident and assertive, surprise her once in a while, this is a sure-fire way to keep your relationship going strong.

Get to know what she likes and what she doesn't like – fast!

A woman of a certain age likes certain things and no longer finds other things as fun as she perhaps once did in her earlier years. Then are some things she just DOESN'T like or tolerate. It is to your advantage if you find out what they are fast and work on them

58

before she turns away from you.

Be interesting for goodness' sake!
The last thing a woman of a certain age wants is to be bored to death by a younger man who has no aptitude for intelligent conversation. We don't mean go out there and read Shakespeare and Plato, but she definitely needs someone with whom she can have a grown up conversation, an intelligent conversation on world matters and other interesting topics that are trending in the news.

You don't have to know every single news headline but having an opinion of your own is important to her. And so is having hobbies that the two of you can share. If you like to live life on the edge with fast sports and do daring things like sky diving, and she is a more subtle and demure kind of woman preferring gentle activities like going to wine tastings or art galleries, then you are going to have to find a middle ground.

This is not saying she won't be keen to try out something new. You may be pleasantly surprised to find that she wants to do something daring and may even end up trying sky diving.

The point is to share your hobbies and activities with one another and make time to do some activities together. On this note, tone down on the clubbing, that is unless you both enjoy going out onto the dance floor to just have a good time.

Instead, focus on building a quality friendship by taking her out on dates to restaurants and movies, places where the two of you can get to know each other better and actually talk. If you do go to the movies, include a romantic walk before or after the movie so that the two of you can simply connect heart to heart.

Invest in a healthy dose of Viagra
Let's face it, the sex is amazing between the two of you and you wouldn't have it any other way. She is a diva and knows how to rock your world and she expects the same from you. Cougars have very healthy sex drives and so being able to satisfy her comes with the territory. If you are able to match up with her and keep her

happy then good for you, but if not, it's nothing to be embarrassed about, get yourself some Viagra and you will be good to go in no time.

If you want to keep your relationship going strong for a long time, you need to keep the fire burning in both your lives. Keep the romance up and don't allow the passion and the excitement you both had at the start to die out. Spice up things from time to time. Go out and do something new, something crazy that you will both enjoy. Do not allow life to get boring because once life gets boring it is easy to fall out of love with each other and move onto the next person.

Cougars get bored easily so make sure you are doing your best at every stage to keep the romance going in your relationship. Cougars are devoted and their commitment levels are high, but they are also wary of cubs that don't know what they want and are simple time wasters. If you don't want her to cut you loose make sure you keep her top priority in your life.

Chapter 8) Dealing With the Cougar/Younger Male Lifestyle

The 21st century has seen men and women the world over come out of their closets and live lifestyles that they have always wanted to live, but have been too scared to live because of what society thought. Thankfully times are changing and men and women are finding it increasingly easier to live as and how they choose to.

The choice to become a cougar and an open cougar at that many decades ago would have been seriously frowned upon, and the woman horribly ostracized and called a train load of names. But thankfully in today's world, the finger pointing and ostracizing has gradually gone down.

Older women and younger men are both questioning fundamentals and challenging the status quo. They have chosen to take a bold step and live stubbornly, embracing the unconventional. Both cubs and cougars are tenaciously breaking down the stereotypes that have long held them captive and are redefining what love is all about.

The cougar/cub lifestyle is exactly that, it is a way of life that older women and younger men have chosen to embrace and live. It is a lifestyle that needs to be understood by the parties involved in order for two people to live in harmony.

Breaking Down the Cougar Lifestyle
The way a person lives is determined by a host of factors. Discussing the cougar lifestyle entails us taking a look at the interests of cougars, their opinions, behaviours and behavioural orientations and their culture.

Let us begin by saying that every cougar is different, and there is no one size fits all when we talk about people. We can talk about generalities but every individual person is different in the end.

The older woman that you meet, her lifestyle will be a reflection of her own unique attitude to life, her individual values and how she views the world as a whole. Her way of life can be very different to your youthful ways and you may find her a bit old fashioned in certain respects. When you meet her and have become a part of her life, do not go into the relationship with the intent of changing her, because all you will meet is resistance and you will not progress any further.

Life with a cougar is much more than just the intimate aspect of things, and in between those intimate moments, you have to put up with her and bear with her. And it is in these moments that you can begin to experience friction and lifestyle differences.

The aspects discussed below are all part and parcel of shaping a person's lifestyle.

Hair and Makeup
The way someone chooses to live their life is a strong reflection of who they are and can forge a sense of being. It gives them a sense of identity. Lifestyle is more important to older women because this is the life they have known and changes can be deeply upsetting and unnerving.

If you find yourself struggling to accept a part of her lifestyle, then instead of outright saying it, take a few days and prepare her before you say it. Don't tell her you don't like the way she does her hair or makeup. She has been doing her hair like that for a long time and you will not get a favourable response that way. Instead, why don't you treat her to a day at the salon and let her get a new look that way? This will not come off as a direct attack but will be taken as a thoughtful and much appreciated gesture.

The same with her makeup; spoil her with a nice day at the spa. On the days that she wears the makeup you like, compliment her and tell she looks beautiful, with time she will pick up on it and change accordingly.

Dress
Not everything about a cougar's lifestyle is voluntary. There are

aspects of her lifestyle that have been pushed upon her because of what society expects from a woman her age, and this is especially true in more conservative places. The way she dresses may be one aspect.

She might have a gorgeous figure but the only time she flaunts it is when she is going out to the bar at night or is within the confines of her own home. She may be comfortable wearing clothes deemed appropriate for her age during the day. You may want her to dress in a particular fashion, like the way you met her in the bar, but she is not willing to do that with you.

How do you deal with this? One way is to tell her how beautiful she looks when she dresses like that. Offer to buy her new clothes and get rid of some of the older ones. Tread carefully on this area though; it is a very sensitive one.

Food
Sometimes when you meet someone, you may not immediately know the intimate details of their life, like whether they are vegan or not. Once the first round of drinks has passed and numbers have been exchanged, and a home run has been scored, it might not be until you decide to go to your first date that you find out more about the woman you are with.

You may discover that she is 100% vegan and doesn't eat all the conventional foods that you like. It's time to kiss the hotdogs, pizzas and hamburgers goodbye for traditional vegan food. Now, while this is an extreme example, it just demonstrates how many times you actually don't know someone.

Food is central to life, it brings people together in so many social settings, and it can be a big issue to deal with in a relationship. If your lifestyle choices are in opposite directions when it comes to this area, then you will have to really sit down and discuss how you are both going to handle it.

It may be a deal breaker for other couples, but it doesn't have to always be. We know couples that cook separately, but are still able to sit down together after both parties have prepared their food. Most couples who have differing food tastes prefer to cook in advance, meal prep, then store the different food items in lunchboxes and pack them in the refrigerator for weekday meals. Where there is a will, there is a way.

This area is more important than most people realize. William Dufty once explained how food has the ability to draw two people who share a mutual interest together. He said, 'I have come to know hundreds of young people who have found that illness or bingeing on drugs and sugar became the doorway to health. Once they re-established their own health, we had in common our interest in food. If one can use that overworked word lifestyle, we shared a sugar free lifestyle. I kept in touch with many of them, met in campuses and communes, through their travels here and abroad and everywhere. One day you meet them in Boston. The next week you run into them in southern California.' The takeaway point from what Dufty was saying is that you never know where you can meet someone and what brings you together.

Political Views
Everybody knows that if you meet someone for the first time, one of the biggest social topics to stay clear of is politics. Political views are not always shared and received with grace. Being much older than you and well-seasoned in life, your woman can hold political views that may go against the views you hold, and believe in.

These views can become a point of great concern when your ideas both go in opposing directions. It's not uncommon to find that many cougars have a very strong sense of what is right and what is wrong and what they want to see changed in the world. With this end in mind, many cougars are very strong women who are not afraid to voice their opinions and have their voices heard in public forums and discussions.

A strong cougar needs to know that you have a mind of your own and you can think and make your own decisions. She needs to be able to sit down and have a political discussion with you and not feel like she is conversing alone.

Religion and Faith
Religion is probably sitting high up as one of the bigger lifestyle issues that will be of great concern to her. With so many religions and faiths to choose from nowadays, you need to ask yourself whether you will be able to conform to what she believes.

If it is too much for you, you have to figure out how you can get around not believing in what she believes in. Faith is a subject similar to politics, which can be a very emotional experience for a woman and very close to her being.

Many women who are particularly devoted to a particular faith may be looking for someone with whom they can share this important aspect of their life. If you know that you cannot share her lifestyle in this regard, it is better to be honest with her from the first day and see how she takes it. If she waves goodbye, take it with grace and move on.

Health and Fitness
In general, cougars tend to take really good care of themselves – how else would they look that amazing at their age? Well, their genes definitely do play a significant role, but we can all agree that health and fitness will certainly play a really big role.

Now, if you are not the early morning bird who sees yourself getting up to jog, then you better find something to do because she isn't going to fancy the idea of giving herself to a man who does not care how he looks.

It is only fair after all. You saw her and liked what you saw, and she saw you and liked what she saw. You have to maintain that physical attraction in order to keep her happy and satisfied. Don't forget that a cougar's life does not revolve around you and if she gets bored with you and starts finding you unattractive, you may find yourself on the short end of the line saying goodbye to one of the best things that ever happened to you.

Come on, get yourself a gym membership and impress her. Show her that you do value yourself and take care of yourself. She will find you irresistible and exceedingly desirous, and well, one thing will lead to another, the level of intimacy will just keep getting better and better. Now if ever there was a reason to look after yourself, isn't this a good enough one?

If a cougar has young children or is looking for someone with whom they can start a family with, then this component is going to play a crucial role in her life. A study done by Case et al. in 2002 demonstrated that children were likely to adopt the lifestyle followed by their parents.

In fact in the study, it was observed that 27% of 0-3 year old children who had mothers who led and practiced healthy lifestyles were themselves likely to adopt a healthy lifestyle and those whose parents did not practice a healthy lifestyle were not a great influence on their children. So if she is looking for a long term partner, then she might be looking for someone with whom she can share common interests and pursuits such as health and wellness with.

Intimacy and Frequency of Sex
A common misconception about cougars is that they are older women who have loose morals. Nothing could be further from the truth. Just because a woman has chosen to adopt the cougar lifestyle does not mean she has loose morals.

When you are coupled with a cougar, you may find that it takes a while before she gives herself up. She is assessing you to see whether or not you are the kind of man that she would like to have sex with. She isn't casual about it and there is nothing casual about her. Making the mistake that she is just an 'easy' woman can cost you the entire relationship. So be careful how you handle this sensitive area.

You should wait to take your cues from her. Leave the ball in her court and allow her to seduce you. Play along and also give her a challenge. Don't make it easy for her. She isn't looking for a man who will hop into bed at any opportunity. She wants to know that you can say no as well. It's all part of the chase, part of the game, part of the fun. The thrill is in the chase.

Another misconception that seems to do the rounds about women of a certain age, is that they stop being sexual after some point. Now this is just one myth that we wish we could take and throw down the drain because if anything, women tend to enjoy sex more as they get better at it with age. Don't be surprised if you find it hard to keep up with her.

Some cougars are not looking for long term 'till death do us apart' commitments. They are simply looking for a friend with benefits. If this is the kind of cougar you have found, then get ready for an explosive love fest.

But what if you struggle to keep up with her? Thanks to latest advancements in medicine and the pharmaceutical industry, there are several aids that can be of help. Viagra, Levitra and Cialis all come to your aid in this department. Don't be underprepared when you meet up with such a cougar. With the use of these pills, you will be able to keep going for hours on end.

Remember to read the instructions on the box before taking any medication. Thankfully you no longer need a doctor's prescription to obtain Viagra, you can simply walk into a pharmacy and purchase the medication.

In general, Cialis and Levitra require a prescription from your doctor. For your own safety, never buy Viagra, Levitra or Cialis from sources that you are not familiar with, especially online. Read up on the best places to obtain the drugs before you go ahead and buy them. They may have side effects as well, so make sure you have read about all the potential side effects before you take them.

Cultural Interests and Leisure Activities
Cultural interests are one area that is often worlds apart when it comes to younger men and older women couplings. Age difference also means that cultural interests are bound to be different. Ideas of

entertainment and social interests an older woman may enjoy might possibly be an area that a younger man is not altogether familiar with, and the same can be said for his musical taste. So going out to theatres and plays may be something she is looking forward to doing but you are completely not into that kind of thing. It can be difficult trying to find middle ground where both of you can share hobbies and interests but it is not impossible.

According to a US survey conducted in 2007, it was discovered that an average person above the age of 15 spends at least 4.9 hours of their time on leisure activities. 2.6 of those hours were spent watching television with only 19 minutes engaged in active correspondence playing a sport or exercise.

These statistics are usually reversed for the older women. You will find that older women spend more time in active engagements and exercise programmes and less and less time watching television. Their favoured leisure activities are jogging, walking, tennis, cycling and for those who enjoy passive activities, they prefer going to the movies and listening to music.

A woman who has developed cultural interests that are wide and varied would need a companion who also shares her passion for such activities. At her age, she isn't looking to hang out in clubs and waste away a night binge drinking. A night of binging is probably not her ideal way to spend an evening.

If you find yourself with such a cougar, take time to listen to the things that she enjoys doing and plan your dates and outings accordingly to her likes and interests. When she is engaged in the activities that she enjoys, you will see her come to life and regain that youthful zeal. You are the key ingredient in the equation.

Children from previous relationship(s)
A cougar's life does not revolve around you and it probably never will. That's just the way it is. A woman who is now secure in her own skin isn't looking to a man to fulfil her needs or for satisfaction. She is complete and finds no reason to go after a man because people tell her she needs one.

She will date when she wants to and whoever she chooses. Women in today's world can now make a comfortable living and pursue their own interests without needing the approval of a husband.

They can provide for themselves and raise their children all by themselves. Things have changed from the days women relied on their husbands for everything, from the food they ate to the clothes they wore. An independent woman is a woman who means business, so it would be beneficial for you to listen to her.

When it comes to her children, you better be aware of the fact that she is as protective over them in much the same way as a lioness is over her cubs. She will not tolerate anyone who does not treat them right or such a person will be cut off immediately and swiftly from her life.

Cubs, if you have decided to date an older woman who has her own children, then you need to understand the fact that you are not going to be her first priority. She has an obligation and a responsibility to look after her children and that is most likely where most of her attention is going to be focused.

You may find yourself coming in second place in her line of priorities. Do not take it personally because that is just the way things are so you had better go on and forget about becoming the number one priority in her life.

When you engage with such a woman do not attempt to change who she is or her love for her children because she can turn on you faster than you can say 'cougar'! And trust us, she will deal with you just as ruthlessly. You will literally be chewed and spit out of her life when it comes to prioritizing her children.

Rather, if you want to win her over, start with her children first. A woman who sees you actively engaging with her children will be moved, and may start to see you as part of her family. In her mind she may start having thoughts like, 'but if he loves my children what is so wrong about me being with him?' The best way to score points with a woman who has her own children is to love her kids first. Don't make it so obvious that you are sucking up to her through the kids. You need to genuinely reach out to the kids and start building a relationship with them as well. If you are planning on being in her life long term you need to have a plan about the children as well, because they will be there in future as well.

Take this as friendly advice, if you start off on a wrong foot with the kids, you may not have a relationship to fight for. Not having an amicable relationship with her children can easily turn the woman against you in a matter of minutes. So you need them to be on your side at all times. All this pertains to children who are still in their younger years.

Dealing with teenagers is a whole different ballgame. Teenagers are mature enough to understand just what is going on. 'Mom has a new boyfriend' – Gag. Teenagers can be strong headed, highly opinionated and at that phase in their lives where they feel territorial and protective over their mom, especially male children. They have potentially been the closest relationship to their mother thus far or have been the 'head' of the home. So when they see another male coming in and closing in on their mom, they can get aggressive.

Teenagers are old enough to understand what is happening between the two of you, so never try and baby them or hide what is happening because you will no sooner make an enemy out of them by assuming that they are too young to handle it.

You, as the incoming male, are not the one responsible to sit down with them and explain to them what is going on between you and their mom, you don't have that right yet, you are still just an outsider to them. Allow their mom to have a sit down with them first. Give them time to accept and think through what is happening. This can be especially hard for teenagers who have never seen their mother dating before.

Teenagers can begin to feel a sense of unease and act out of fear of what could happen to the world that they have grown up knowing. Teenagers with single parents generally have an unspoken fear that their only parent will abandon them or leave them. You need to encourage their mother to be as transparent and honest as she can with them.

If you are looking for a long term relationship with their mother, then you definitely need to start looking at involving the children a little bit more in your activities together.

You are also going to have to develop your own relationship with the children before you can even start thinking of marrying their mother if that is where you want your relationship to go. Involving her children is easy and most activities you do together can be enjoyed by her family such as going to the movies or to the beach.

You also need to remember that if a woman introduces you to her children it is because she is now comfortable enough with you to invite you to share this special part of her life. Do not take this for granted. Show her how much you value being a part of her life and treat her and her kids well.

One way to score points with the children is for them to see you treating their mother with respect and the courtesy she deserves. Open her car door, hold doors for her, and carry heavy things for her. When they see the small things you do to show you care for her, and when they see how you make her so happy, their hostile view of you can begin to change and soften.

You need to do things that show you are man and can be in charge without overtly seeming like you are trying to dominate. You can do this by volunteering to take everyone out for some fun and games.

If the woman's children are boys, you may want to organise something exciting for you and boys to show them how 'cool' you are. Spend time with the boys getting to know them. Do things with them that perhaps their own father never got to do with them, things that will make them want to see you again. This is one of the first ways you can start to break the ice and get through to the male children.

To the girls if she has any daughters, you will need to treat them with courtesy and respect. Don't make them feel uncomfortable by being too playful with them. This may not settle well with mom. Remember you are still a stranger in the house and she has every right to feel protective over her girls. So just be mindful about how you choose to interact with her daughters.

If your woman's children are older and in college, then treat them like the adults they are with the respect that they deserve. These children may be more understanding than both toddlers and teenagers but they can also be the ones who can give you the greatest challenge.

The problem comes when you are slightly older than they are and they feel like they do not need to respect you. It can be really hard to have to face this, because their mother cannot do anything about it. You will simply have to toughen up and show them why you want to be with their mother and how well you can take care of her and her needs.

It is really hard for children to dispute with someone who makes their mother happy. Often times this is the one key element that will allow children to give way and give their blessing to their mother's relationship, when they see how much you make her happy regardless of your age.

Then again, after all is said and done, there is the easier road of simply not disclosing your age to any one of the children. If the both of you think that this may be best then you don't have an obligation to tell the children that you are younger than their mom. This is in fact the route that most cougar/cub relationships take. It helps to avoid the drama and confusion that may take place.

Biological Issues
Following the topic of children, and seeing the direction your own relationship may be heading with your woman, you may begin to ask yourself whether or not you would like to have children with her. Now this is where things can get a little interesting in your relationship. A cougar can be a woman of any age who enjoys and

pursues the company and associations of young men but the term is often referring to a mature woman who is 40 years and above.

Most women aged 40 and older are not looking to have children, if they already have children of their own, or simply no longer want to have any more children. By the age of 40 most women are done giving birth.

However, because of the prevalent culture women across the world have adopted today, many women are getting married later and later, with the average age for a woman to get married in developed countries hovering around 29.9 years. That's almost 30, so you could potentially meet up with a cougar that has never been married and doesn't have children and is looking to start a family.

However let us look at the complex issue of taking your relationship to the next level, where you are thinking of settling down with her, starting and raising a family and she is well, 'been there, done that' kind of thing. How do you deal with such a situation and how best do you approach her with this idea of starting a family?

First and foremost you are going to have to talk about this way in advance before you ever pop the 'will you marry me?' question, lest you pop the question and find out much later on that she has no intentions of having children again. This would leave you in a bit of a muddle, wouldn't it?

You need to sit down with her and ask her what she thinks about the two of you settling down together, possibly getting married and starting a family together. You need to be as direct and honest as you can here. And be prepared to hear anything. You may find out that perhaps she has had her tubes tied and hence can no longer have biological children of her own. Well, this is a first step to determining if you still want to stay together although it is no longer a deal breaker in today's world where there are many options to have children.

Okay, so you have established that you both want children, but she is not able to carry children anymore, what now?

Surrogate Mothers
The idea of a surrogate mother is not new anymore but it is still far from a lot of people's minds. In the event that your woman is unable to carry your children, you can opt to have another woman carry your child.

Let us take a quick look at what surrogacy is and how it works.

What is surrogacy?
Surrogacy is when another woman carries the biological child of another couple. In this process, the surrogate mother has the fertilised egg artificially inseminated into her womb and will then carry the child to term until it is born. When the child is born the surrogate mother will give that child to its respective parents.

There are two ways in which surrogacy can take place. One, either the sperm of the father-to-be is inserted into the surrogate woman's uterus which would mean that the surrogate mother also becomes the biological mother of the child. The second manner which is known as gestational surrogacy, involves the surrogate mother being inseminated with an egg that is already fertilised (by your sperm and your partner's egg), and in this process she is just the host carrier for the child.

In America, there are estimations that in each state there are on average up to nine children born via surrogacy every year. The Council for Responsible Genetics hasn't disclosed any statistics yet, but some physicians estimate that between 2004 and 2008 as many as 5000 children were born from this process.

THE PRESENCE OF OTHER MEN IN HER LIFE
Men by nature do not like to be compared to other men, no matter if the man is a previous lover, husband, boyfriend or anything else in between. It is an unsettling matter in a man's mind to even imagine his woman with another man. Yes, you may be younger than her, but it doesn't mean you are immune to her past. Her past is an area that will surface at some time in your relationship. There

must be a boundary drawn around your own relationship that will protect it from the past.

If there are children in the house, i.e. children from a previous marriage, then you cannot do anything about the children's father's name being raised from time to time in conversation. Things may get awkward if ever you have to meet the previous husband.

However, what you have to remember in times like these is that you have the best thing that he let go. When he is around you, make sure you show him that you are man enough to look after her needs and you are not simply a child no matter how much he may want to play the age card. Hit him where it hurts. You have the best thing he let go. Prove it to him; treat her like a queen when he is around. Shower her with love in his presence. You'll leave him wondering why he ever let your woman go.

When you start to date a cougar it isn't time to sit back and relax. As a man you have to show that you are not with her because you want anything from her, you are with her because she is your choice and your desire.

If you want to break the stereotypes that people have about cubs, then you need to show people that you can stand alone as your own man and can do your own thing. This is one way in which the cougar you are with is going to respect you more. No woman likes knowing that her man is below her or isn't putting his all into developing himself. Every woman likes seeing her man succeed and she will cheer you on and encourage and build you to be and do all that you can be.

If ever there was a reason to rise up and build something with your own hands it's so that she can be proud of you and have something to say when those who like making snide remarks start talking. She will be able to say exactly what you do for a living without having to glide over that part or change the subject out of embarrassment. Furthermore you yourself as a man will start to feel worthy of her and will start to feel like more of a man that is able to look after and meet the needs of his woman.

Not every cougar is a woman of loose morals. This is first and foremost a notion that you need to eliminate before you can progress with your cougar of choice. She may have had several men in her past that you may need to come to terms with but that is something that you will have to deal with and not her. You shouldn't bring up her past lovers in much the same way as she does not want to hear about your past escapades with younger women. Let the past be that, the past for both of you.

If you feel like you would like to address the people that were in both your lives in order to move on with your relationship as a couple, then you need to discuss it at the right time and the right place. In the event of an argument do not bring up comparisons of past lovers no matter how tempted you may be to throw that in her face. It will only serve to fuel the fire and possibly lead to a split and a ridge from which neither of you can come back from. The best way to be safe is to ask her if she would like to talk about her past. If she agrees to then she will talk about her past, if not then leave it at that.

Respect her privacy. In much the same way, do not volunteer information about your past unless she specifically asks. And even if she does ask, what good does it do for your current relationship to tell her all the gory details or intimate details of your past girlfriends? Find a way around it without making her feel like you are comparing her to your former lovers. Avoid statements like, 'Oh Shelly used to do ABC for me, but oh well, I don't get that anymore now' it is both insulting to the woman that you are currently with now, and that you would even dare think of another woman while she is sitting right in front of you is very disrespectful.

When you decide to engage in the cougar/cub lifestyle, prepare to have a great time but also prepare to deal with a whole lot as well.

Final Thoughts

We have seen how the world is slowly but surely changing its perception and stereotypical views of what cougars and cubs are all about. Like with all cultural norms that must be broken and changed, it has taken some time, and there is still a long way to go before the negative connotation that is associated with the terms disappear.

Top take away lessons from this Cougar Dating Guide:

1. EMBRACE THE TERMS COUGAR AND CUB IN ORDER TO BREAK STEREOTYPES

The first thing we learnt and saw in this book is how cougars and cubs need to embrace and own this kind of lifestyle. You cannot live unsure of where you stand as Cougar Life founder Claudia Opdenkelder emphasised that, 'if you are on the fence about whether or not you think you are a cougar or not, then you probably aren't one.'

You can't live with an undecided mind. You have to grab life by the horns and enjoy every moment of being a cougar. The same goes with being a cub. You have got to know where you stand. It's okay if you like going back and forth between younger and older women. In fact, you are not alone. One of the questions that was asked of cubs as part of the survey conducted by popular cub and Cougared founder Oliver Jameson, was 'Are older women your only preference?'

****

52% of cubs said they date older women and younger women equally
32% of cubs admitted that they mostly date cougars for the fun and the 'cougar experience'
17% of cubs said they dated older women exclusively
****

And it was interesting to see the responses. As you can see, the answers are across the board, with some men preferring to spice it up and go between the age ranges and some only being there for the experience.

There are cubs out there who enjoy being with older women for a season to simply learn some tricks, while for others it is for the long run. You don't have to throw yourself into a category. If you have never been in a cougar/cub relationship and you have been reading this book in order to learn how to go about it, our advice is you don't have to try and fit into any one sole category. Just go with the flow and enjoy the ride.

You don't have to know everything all at once, but definitely what you have picked up from this book will carry you a long way. The takeaway lesson from Chapter 1 - Embrace this lifestyle and own it!

2. WHOEVER SAID LIFE BEGINS AT 40 WAS RIGHT!

The advantages for cougars are unparalleled as we saw clearly in Chapter 2. Whoever said life begins at 40 was right indeed and cougars will be able to testify to the truth of that statement.

A woman, who has reached a certain age, doesn't really care much for societal norms and customs and really couldn't be bothered. They have come to the realisation that life is too short to waste away trapped by what other people think and why be alone if you can be with someone who worships the ground you tread upon? Hey, if it is good for the gander it is also good for the goose right? What men are allowed to do, women should also be allowed to do without being made to feel remorseful or ashamed.

A young man can reawaken the love and passion in a woman and make her youthful again. This is the power that you as a cub can bring into the life of a cougar. Not only do you bring a rejuvenating spirit into her life but you reawaken the desires that are hidden in her and get to learn a few tricks here and there. It's a give and take relationship. The main takeaway points from this chapter are the numerous reasons why a cougar should enjoy being with a younger man.

3. WHERE THERE IS A WILL, THERE IS A WAY

Every relationship, regardless of whether it is between a 45 year old man and a 30 year old woman, or a 45 year old woman and a 30 year old man, goes through challenges.

Challenges, disagreements, misunderstandings are part and parcel of every relationship out there. There is no couple that can stand up and honestly say, 'In our relationship, we have never had a disagreement, a misunderstanding, we've only ever had a perfect harmony and union.' No, in every relationship, and with every couple there are bound to be mountains that must be overcome.

Cougars understand this because they probably have been in more relationships longer than their counterparts. So when they encounter challenges with their younger beau, they are not disheartened greatly, but they look for solutions as to how best they can make their relationship work. And the point to take away from this chapter is that, 'Where there is a will, there will always be a way.'

4. THE BEST KEPT SECRET TO FASTRACKING YOUR LIFE IS BEING WITH A COUGAR

Cubs of every age enter cougar/cub relationships with a goal and a purpose in mind. Now every cub is different in much the same way as every cougar is different. But the advantages that come with being in such a relationship come to one and all. There is much to be gotten from being with an older woman. Almost every cub who has ever been in a relationship with a cougar before will tell you that they learnt something from her, and more often than not it was in the bedroom.

However there are more things than just bedroom tricks to learn that have been outlined and discussed in great depth and detail in this chapter.

The takeaway point from Chapter 4 has been that older women relationships almost always leave a younger man for the better. He finds himself more confident, more experienced and more assured of himself. If you want to fast track your way in life, then dating an older woman is one sure fire way of doing it!

5. YOUR ATTITUDE DETERMINES YOUR ALTITUDE

While the benefits of being with a cougar almost always far outweigh the disadvantages, it doesn't mean that the disadvantages do not exist. They are there and they will need you as the cub to work through them in order to get the most out of your cougar experience.

Your experience and what you will take away from this relationship is all dependent on your attitude and how you enter the relationship. You have now learnt how a cougar thinks and what she expects, so going against that grain could land you in serious trouble.

If you want things to go well with you then you need to heed the advice in this book. Take away point, your attitude will take you further and cause you to learn all you can from a cougar. Let her teach you, she has much that you can learn.

6. KEEP YOUR EYES OPEN!

Our celebrity cougar/cub examples showed us how you can meet your cougar anywhere. There is no set place where you can say, 'this is the place I am going to meet her.' It can happen anywhere and at any time. It doesn't matter whether you are in the supermarket, petrol station, bar or nightclub or even in your workplace. As we saw in Chapter 6, keeping your eyes open is vital. So keep a good lookout and let nature take its course!

7. THE X FACTOR OF ATTRACTION

Physical attraction or sexual attraction, whatever attraction you two might have, the key to remember is that you two were drawn to one another. However, we saw that this attraction is not enough to seal the deal. There is more that goes on in the mind of a cougar than just the physical attraction. There are steps you need to take before she notices you and after she notices you. For some, it might be a complete makeover that is needed to get your game face on. Whatever it is that you need in order for her to notice you, it is spelt out in this chapter. This chapter shared with you the importance of grooming and how to treat a lady.

8. YOU NEED TO MAINTAIN WHAT YOU HAVE OBTAINED

Everything you have learnt right up until this point should have given you a 100% success rate with the cougar that caught your eye.

By the time you get to this chapter you have probably done pretty well with your online searches and perhaps have even had success in other scenarios attracting and getting attention from cougars. It has been all fun and games up until this moment, but now you have to do more than just have fun with your cougar.

Now you need to learn how to keep her. You have learnt just how restless cougars can get and if bored they can easily walk away. Now, it gets a little tougher and you need to learn to maintain what you have obtained.

Looking at a Ferrari and admiring it in a car dealership or an auto floor is exhilarating. Everyone is surrounding the car and wishes they could own it. However you are the lucky one who can afford that Ferrari and you buy it. Everyone now admires you in the streets and it makes you feel good....the only downside is the ridiculous monthly payments that you must make to keep the car running smoothly. You have to service the car as often as recommended and use the best parts on it; you can't by a Ferrari from a high end dealership and expert it to be serviced from a back yard dealership. You will do more harm than good to your car.

The same goes with a sophisticated cougar. You saw her and you liked what you saw. But see, it wasn't just you who was looking at her. Several other cubs had their eyes on her, but because of the tips you have learnt from this book you beat them to it and won her over much to their dismay.

So now she is yours, but you see, if you won her over by taking her out to dine at fancy places you cannot expect to take her to a rundown establishment or a corner food hut and expect her to stay.

81

If you won her by being romantic, buying flowers, expensive chocolates, then you had better keep doing the same otherwise she is going to see past your first attempts.

Remember cougars are like free spirits, free to roam as they please. If she isn't being treated like she knows she deserves she will leave you, trust us on this one. So the takeaway point of Chapter 8 is that in order to keep her interested you have to keep doing what got her in the first place and more! Don't stop!

9. IT WAS ALL FUN AND GAMES UNTIL REALITY HIT

Dating is fun. Who doesn't like the thrill of the chase? Being wooed, chased, courted, and wined and dined? Both cougar and cub alike love it.

The first stages of every relationship are always full of exciting new things, getting to know someone is always exhilarating. The emotions are still running high, the attraction is real and it's mutual and is strong, and your mind is already exploring the future. In the heat of the moment there are some important lifestyle issues that are easy to overlook as two people get to know each other. Lifestyle issues that can get side-lined by the passion that is flaring between the two of you, it's all so very easy.

When reality decides to knock on the door that is when things can start getting a bit hard and you need to take a step back and really assess the situation you find yourself in and what you are going to do especially if you are planning on going to the next level with her.

All the various lifestyle issues that can be hard to deal with are discussed in this chapter in sufficient depth. The takeaway point of Chapter 9 is that real issues will have to be dealt with but there is nothing that cannot be figured out. You don't have to have everything sorted out before you move onto the next level but you have to start thinking seriously about how to handle some of the pertinent issues that you may be faced with. And luckily for you we have spelt out and given you tools to help you get started on working on to have a successful future with your woman.

Conclusion

Before we complete this book, we'd like to leave you with some important and valuable tips on how to sustain your relationship with your cougar. These tips below are by far the top tips you should remember if you want to take your relationship all the way.

1. TRULY LISTEN WHEN SHE SPEAKS

The fastest way to lose the respect and attention of a cougar is to show that you are not interested in truly listening to her. Do not try to finish off her sentences, just listen, and hear her out. In order to build a really long lasting relationship, you will need to learn how to communicate. Communication isn't all about speaking. Your body language also makes up part of your communication. What is your body language saying to her? Are you listening to her with your arms crossed across your chest? That says, I am listening but am trying to keep a distance between us. Communicate your needs, your problems and your thoughts to her as well. On a daily basis set aside time where the two of you connect with each other after a long day. Touch is the best way of reconnecting. Hug, kiss, make love; it serves to bring you closer every day and keeps you connected to each other. When you are with her, put the phone on silent and focus on her. Give her your undivided attention.

2. DO SOMETHING NICE FOR HER EVERYDAY

Make it a habit to do something nice for her everyday. It doesn't have to be something big or something that costs money; she will appreciate even the tiniest gesture. Make the bed, make breakfast, clean the house, take out the trash, load the dishwasher, buy her flowers, write her a note and place it somewhere she is likely to see at work, take her out to lunch, and make dinner. The list is endless. There are hundreds of things you could do for her on a daily basis. To make it easier for you, take about twenty minutes one day, just sit and brainstorm at least thirty different ideas of things you could do for her and write the list down. For the next thirty days take each one of the things you have listed down and perform it until you have completed the thirty days, then sit down again and come up with a new list for the next month or simply repeat the current one.

3. BE PASSIONATE ABOUT BEING WITH HER

Guys, she expects you to romance her and sweep her off her feet. Don't become a bore after you have her. You have to keep the romance alive and the fire burning. Express your love to her, tell her to her face that you love her and mean it. Surprise her, take her out to out-of-the way places that are not her usual dining spots, places you are sure she will like, or if you are the adventurous type and are confident you can pull it off, how about a candle lit dinner for two by the beach? If you can't cook, then buy the best take out you can afford and make it special. Be a gentleman, bring flowers for her and make it a memorable date.

4. HAVE A PLAN FOR YOUR LIFE

Cubs, no cougar likes a man who isn't responsible. If you want her to respect you and stay with you, then you need to get your act together and get yourself a place of your own and start paying some bills. If you want her to take you seriously, then you need to show her that you take yourself seriously and that you have a plan for your life and are working on it day by day. No woman likes the idea of a man who depends on his parents for his upkeep; it's not sexy at all and can be a deal breaker. Remember that cougars have their own money and are not looking for your money. She isn't worried about the financial side of things but rather is thinking how much of a liability you can prove to be if you don't have your own work to concentrate on. She is not your ticket to a better financial life so don't approach her like that.

5. LAUGH

Nothing breaks the ice more than a good hearty laugh. Laugh at everything and nothing. Make it a habit to laugh together everyday. Laughter is by far the easiest way to make her adore you. A cougar needs a man who can make her laugh at life and at the silly things. She will love you all the more for making her laugh on a daily basis and she will feel your absence when you are not there. You will become a very important part of her life very easily through laughter, so don't forget to make her laugh boys.

6. REMEMBER YOUR MANNERS

Don't forget to say please and thank you. The small things within a relationship can make the biggest difference. In line with learning how to do something nice everyday, remembering your manners is about as base level as things get in a relationship because it's so easy to take each other for granted and forget to take time to appreciate each other. Next time you think 'But she knows that I'm grateful' and you want to skip it, say it. Thank her for preparing dinner, for cleaning the house; tell her how much you love her and how much you feel like the luckiest guy in the entire world for having her to yourself.

7. STOP CARING WHAT PEOPLE THINK

Spending time worrying what people think about your relationship and voicing it to her can end up wearing her down. She is already aware of the age gap and the relationship complex; she doesn't need to hear it from you. She probably gets to hear about it more than you do so cut it out with the age gap stories when you are with her. And for goodness sake don't mention her age when you are in the company of other people. They say you never ask a lady her age for a reason, so don't cross the boundary and don't be the one who brings the age story to the table. What others think should not be the decisive factor in your relationship. Let them talk but don't allow it to break into your relationship and take center stage.

8. DON'T PUT UNREALISTIC EXPECTATIONS ON YOUR RELATIONSHIP

It is easy to get into your relationship guns blazing thinking you are going to be hooking up and having sex all day every day. The reality of the situation is while she is likely to have a high sex drive, you probably will NOT be able to have sex all the time. Have a realistic expectation of your relationship. If you have established a friends with benefits kind of relationship, then it is easy to have sex every day as long as that is the agreement, but for the common cougar/cub relationship, you might have to keep things a bit more on the realistic side. Another point to add here is the expectations you each have of each other. What she expects of you and what you expect of her. She will expect you to be a gentleman regardless of your age and to treat her accordingly.

9. BE HONEST

Honesty is always the best policy in a relationship. If she asks you something then she expects you to answer it as honestly as you can. She isn't a young girl who you have to shield and protect for fear that she might get hurt by the truth. No, tell it to her as it is. Tell her the truth and don't hide it from her because she will find out, and trust us when she finds out it won't be pretty if it's something really bad that you have been keeping from her. Remember, cougars are not holding onto you, the minute they get bored they can easily let go of you, so you better play your cards right. As your relationship begins to progress and you start getting to know each other better, don't be afraid to show her what's inside your closet. She can handle it.

10. DON'T TRY TO RULE OVER HER

Remember, cougars are strong independent women who have their lives in order and don't need a young man trying to tell them what to do. This is the last thing she wants and will not tolerate it. She would rather cut you out of her life than have you tell her what to do. If you are looking for a way to get kicked out of her life faster than you can say 'cougar' then just try telling her what to do and see what happens. This is not to say she isn't open to hear what you may have to say, she is, as long as it is within reasonable bounds. When it comes to her life, don't try to tell her how to live her life, let it be.

11. DON'T BE AFRAID TO MAKE MISTAKES

Come on, this is one of the things that makes us all human beings, the ability to make mistakes and get over them. Don't be afraid to make mistakes when you are with her. She isn't expecting you to be perfect. More than anything she understands men better than you probably think and might understand the things you are struggling with more than you know. You don't have to be shy about the things you are going through. Talk to her, communicate, you will get through it together. She has much to teach you and you have much to learn from her. Let her help you and don't be resentful if she tells you what to do, because more often than not, her advice is pretty solid. When all is said and done, do learn from those mistakes and move on.

12. BE TRUSTWORTHY

Nothing destroys relationships faster than infidelity. If you are going to be with her, then be with her only. Don't two time her or double date at the same time. Even worse, don't date a younger woman and her at the same time; you are digging your own grave if you do this. Why even bother dating a younger woman when you have the full package in a cougar? Seriously boys, think about that. If you want to be with her then you need to show her that you are serious and only want her and no one else. Cougars are very territorial and get jealous very easily. They want you to worship the ground they tread upon and made to feel like the queens they are. A woman of a certain age has reached that time in her life where she is in her prime and wants to be treated like a goddess. Remember, if you want the best out of her, then you need to treat her right. In order to get the goods you need to be good.

13. FORGIVE EACH OTHER

Holding on to grudges is probably the number one relationship breaker around. Don't hold onto something she said about you being immature and irresponsible. Take it as a challenge to grow and become a more responsible man. Prove it to her. At the same time mind the things you say to her. Cougars are tough and strong women, but they still have a very sensitive part and can sometimes still carry girlhood insecurities. The words you choose to use with her can see her either blossom or wither. Remember, a cougar is still a woman, and women are like flowers. If you want to see her bloom, treat her right. Let your words be like gentle rain falling into her life. You can have the woman of your dreams. It's all up to how you treat her.

When all is said and done just remember too that there has never been one place that people say, 'this is it! This is the place all hook-ups are made.' No, it doesn't work that way. It would be wrong of us to sit here and tell you that if you go and stand by the street corner, a cougar will notice you. Perhaps that is not where you are meant to meet your cougar, perhaps you were meant to meet her in an elevator during rush hour. Nobody can tell you what you should and shouldn't do.

All we can do is to present to you the research we have done and the successes and failures of others. Learning from others is a far simpler task than having to experience everything first hand yourself. Take the advice of others and use it to your own advantage. Perhaps you didn't even have an idea or clue as to how to go about finding a cougar and where to find one, but now you have more than ten websites to choose from and subscribe to. Now you know where else other than bars and nightclubs you can meet your cougar.

Once again, we go back to our celebrity examples who demonstrate that love can find you anywhere and at any time. If at first you don't succeed in one area, don't give up. If after having joined one website you find out that you are not getting any responses to your messages, perhaps change your profile picture to a more attractive one and change the website. You might be targeting the wrong cougars because you are on the wrong platform.

There is no shame in knowing what you want from the relationship before you go looking. Going back to Oliver Jameson's 2011 survey, when cubs were asked what is was exactly that they were looking for, these were their varying replies:

- 34% casual dating or open relationship
- 24% one-night stand or no strings attached sex
- 23% a normal girlfriend who just happens to be older
- 11% to be taken care of by a rich older woman
- 8% long term commitment with the potential of marriage in mind

It is important to know that there are platforms specifically tailored to meet each and every one of the needs listed above. There are websites notorious for being great hook up places for those looking for one-night stands. But you see, not everyone is looking for just a one-night stand.

There are cubs in the 8% who are looking for a potential 'till death do us part' commitment. Website creators respond accordingly and there are sites for those who seek such relationships. So if at first you don't succeed with a site, get to know what the site caters to and if it is not what you are looking for, you can simply leave that website and join one which satisfies your needs.

With all the tools, tips and guidelines you have received and learned in this book, you are now set and ready to go out to cougarville and conquer! So, onwards cubs the future is yours for the taking! Carpe Diem, seize the day!

Resources

Note: these resources were correct at the time of printing. However, the internet changes rapidly so some links might no longer work when you read this book. Unfortunately this cannot be helped and is out of our control.

TOP COUGAR DATING WEBSITES

USA Cougar Dating Sites
www.dateacougar.com
www.cougarlife.com
www.cougared.com
www.cougardates.com
www.playcougar.com
www.urbancougar.com
www.cougarfling.com
www.cougarsmeet.com
www.becougar.com
www.cougar911.com
www.playcougar.com

UK Cougar Dating Sites
www.dateacougar.uk
www.toyboy.com
www.toyboywarehouse.com

COUGAR YOUTUBE VIDEOS
https://www.youtube.com/watch?v=0kdmo7cnSy4
https://www.youtube.com/watch?v=GmM3IhMJ9oo
https://www.youtube.com/watch?v=5Y8w3LBUCc4
https://www.youtube.com/watch?v=tNMW0nhCg18
https://www.youtube.com/watch?v=FB3maaWrMuY

COUGAR RELATED ARTICLES

http://www.cougared.com/report/

http://www.leadingdatingsites.co.uk/cougar-dating.htm

http://www.cougardate.co.uk/

http://www.today.com/health/reasons-why-younger-guys-fall-older-women-I283710

http://www.chicagonow.com/love-lawyer/2011/11/how-to-attract-a-cougar-and-keep-her-purring/

https://en.wikipedia.org/wiki/Age_disparity_in_sexual_relationships

http://www.modernfamilysurrogacy.com/page/surrogacy_statistics

www.ingramcontent.com/pod-product-compliance
Lightning Source LLC
La Vergne TN
LVHW051704080426
835511LV00017B/2715